Mass Communication

STUDIES IN
SOCIOLOGY

Mass Communication

A Sociological Perspective

CHARLES R. WRIGHT

National Science Foundation

Random House · New York

Library of Congress Catalog Card Number: 59-14519

Manufactured in the United States of America

PREFACE

This Study is not a miniature textbook, the sociology of mass communication is too new and complex to be condensed into a hundred or so pages of textbook "lessons." Rather, the book is intended as an introduction to this new field. Each chapter presents to the reader a major subdivision of the field, at various levels of detail and selectivity.

The book begins with a challenge: after exploring those characteristics that distinguish mass communications from other forms, it invites the reader to apply one sociological orientation—functional analysis—to the determination of their social effects. Chapter 2 employs a broader, more descriptive, approach, giving an overview of several foreign communications systems against which our own can be compared. Chapter 3 on the sociology of the audience, is narrower in focus but more detailed. Here are summarized some of the major research findings about one aspect of mass communication—the link between the mass media and face-to-face communication in the society. Chapter 4 supplies examples of qualitative and quantitative analyses of mass media content. It focuses first on studies of the kinds of characters presented as heroes and villains in our popular culture. Then it examines the content of an average week of television broadcasts in metropolitan America. The final chapter returns to the topic introduced in Chapter I—the social effects of mass communication. Here speculation is tempered with empirical research findings. Not all social effects are considered, of course; but those discussed provide an introduction to the rich and complex problems for sociological theory and research that are posed by this topic.

For the reader who wishes more information about such other aspects of mass communication as research methods, international communication, and public opinion, a list of selected readings is appended to the Study.

It is my pleasure to acknowledge an indebtedness to several friends and colleagues. I have benefited from thoughtful and critical readings of the manuscript by Herbert H. Hyman, Mary E. W. Goss, Raymond J. Murphy, and Charles H. Page. A direct and immeasurably important intellectual source for my sociological perspective on mass communications is the training and research experience I have enjoyed under three masters of the subject: Herbert H. Hyman, Paul F. Lazarsfeld, and Robert K. Merton. None of these generous people, of course, is in any way responsible for whatever defects the Study may have.

CHARLES R. WRIGHT

CONTENTS

Mass Communication

1

The Nature
and Functions
of Mass Communication

What is Mass Communication?

Communication is the process of transmitting meaning
between individuals. For human beings the process is both
fundamental and vital. It is fundamental insofar as all
human society—primitive to modern—is founded on man's
capacity to transmit his intentions, desires, feelings, knowledge, and experience from person to person. It is vital
insofar as the ability to communicate with others enhances
the individual's chances for survival, while its absence is
generally regarded as a serious form of personal pathology.
Occasionally children have been discovered who, having
spent their earliest years in isolation from other human
beings, have lacked verbal communication experience.
These isolated children behaved in ways little different
from other animals, and shared their lack of cultural
control over the natural environment. Not until the rudi-
ments of human communication were established with
these individuals did they enter into social relations with
other humans and acquire the cultural advantages which
most persons accept as a birthright.[1]

It seems inevitable that a process so fundamental and
vital to human survival should, in whole or in part, have
been a subject for study throughout history. Indeed, from
antiquity to modern times the process of human communication has attracted the attention of a long line of

authors employing a rich assortment of intellectual orientations, including the artistic, the philosophical, and the
political. Only recently, however, has communication become a topic for scientific investigation and, more par-
ticularly, for inquiry by social scientists in certain fields,
especially anthropology, political science, psychology, and
sociology. In keeping with this latest trend, the present
Study assumes a *sociological* orientation to the subject.

But the entire field of human communication is not
the focus of our work. From the wide span of methods by
which meanings are transmitted in human societies, ranging
from the most primitive gestures to the most sophisticated
electronic techniques, a small but important segment has
been selected—that segment of symbolic transmission commonly identified as *mass communication*. What is presented
here is an initial step toward a sociological analysis of the
process and social consequences of mass communication.

To start, we need a working definition of mass communication. We need to describe a few of the characteristics of mass communication that help to distinguish it
from other forms of human communication. Then, in
the second section of this chapter, we speculate about some
of the social consequences of the mass form of communication.

In popular usage the phrase "mass communication"
evokes images of television, radio, motion pictures, newspapers, comic books, etc. But these technical instruments
should not be mistaken for the *process* with which we are
concerned. Mass communication, as it is used in this Study,
is *not* simply a synonym for communication by means
of radio, television, or any other modern technique.
Although modern technology is essential to the process,
its presence does not always signify mass communication.
The nation-wide telecast of a political convention is mass
communication; the closed-circuit telecast over which
industrial assembly line operations are monitored by an
engineer is not. Or, to take a more mundane example, a
Hollywood motion picture is mass communication; a home
movie of vacation scenes is not. Both media in each

example use similar modern techniques—electronic transmission of images in one case, film recording of scenes in the other. Nevertheless one of each pair does not qualify as mass communication. The point is perhaps labored: it is not the technical components of modern communications systems that distinguish them as mass media; rather, mass communication is a special kind of communication involving distinctive operating conditions, primary among which are the nature of the audience, of the communication experience, and of the communicator.

NATURE OF THE AUDIENCE   Mass communication is directed toward a relatively large, heterogeneous, and anonymous audience. Hence, messages addressed to specific individuals are not customarily regarded as mass communications. Such a criterion excludes letters, telephone calls, telegrams, and the like from our Study. This does not deny that the postal and telecommunications systems play an important role in the communications network of any society. Most certainly they do. Indeed, in some instances they are often linked to the mass media, performing vital functions in the overall communications process, aiding, for example, in the spread of information to areas of the society or segments of the population not reached by the mass media. But the term mass communication is reserved for other activities.

Each of the criteria cited here for a mass audience is relative and needs further specification. For example, what size audience is "large"? Extreme cases are easily classified: a television audience of millions is large; a lecture audience of several dozen is small. But what about an audience of four or five hundred people listening to an evangelist speaking in a tent? Obviously the cutting point must be an arbitrary one. A tentative definition would consider as "large" any audience exposed during a short period of time and of such a size that the communicator could not interact with its members on a face-to-face basis.

The second requirement is that the audience be heterogeneous. Thus communications directed toward an exclusive or elite audience are excluded. For example, the transmission of news (by whatever means) exclusively to members of a governing party or ruling class is not mass communication. Mass-communicated news is offered to an aggregation of individuals occupying a variety of positions within the society—persons of many ages, both sexes, many levels of education, from many geographic locations, and so on.

Finally, the criterion of anonymity means that the individual audience members generally remain personally unknown to the communicator. It does not mean that they are socially isolated. Indeed, there is growing evidence that much of mass communication exposure takes place within the setting of small social groups; and even when physically isolated the audience member, of course, is linked to a number of primary and secondary social groupings which can modify his reaction to the message. But, with respect to the communicator, the message is addressed "to whom it may concern."

NATURE OF THE COMMUNICATION EXPERIENCE   Mass communications may be characterized as public, rapid, and transient. They are public because, insofar as the messages are addressed to no one in particular, their content is open for public surveillance. They are rapid because the messages are meant to reach large audiences within a relatively short time, or even simultaneously—unlike works of fine art, which may be examined at leisure over centuries. They are transient because they are usually intended to be consumed immediately, not to enter into permanent records. Of course there are exceptions, such as film libraries, radio transcriptions, and kinescope recordings, but customarily the output of the mass media is regarded as expendable.

As we will note in more detail later, the nature of the communication experience may have important social consequences. Its public character may make it a subject for community censorship and control through legislation, public opinion, and other social mechanisms. The simultaneity of the message—its ability to reach large audiences in a brief time span—suggests potential social power in its impact. Mass communication's transiency has led, in some instances, to an emphasis on timeliness and sensation in content.

NATURE OF THE COMMUNICATOR   Mass communication is organized communication. Unlike the lone artist or writer, the "communicator" in mass media works through a complex organization embodying an extensive division of labor and an accompanying degree of expense. One need only call to mind the vast institutional structure surrounding the production of a Hollywood film or the bureaucratic complexity of television network production to recognize the dissimilarities between such communication and traditional earlier forms. Similarly, modern communications are more costly. For example, it has been estimated that a TV station, say for college productions, would cost approximately $265,000 to equip and another $220,000 annually to operate.[2] Production costs for a network fifteen-minute newscast have been reported as $3400.[3]

These distinctions are not merely academic, but have important consequences for the communication process. The complexity of modern mass media has moved the creative artist many stages away from his final product. And the production expense is decreasing the access to the media of communication for persons wishing to reach the public.

To summarize, recent technological developments have made possible a new form of human communication: mass communication. This new form can be distinguished from older types by the following major characteristics: it is directed toward relatively large, heterogeneous, and anonymous audiences; messages are transmitted publicly, often timed to reach most audience members simultaneously, and are transient in character; the communicator tends to be, or to operate within, a complex organization that may involve great expense. These conditions of communication have important consequences for the traditional activities which are carried out by communicators in society—some of which are considered below.

Some Aims and Functions of Mass Communication

Harold Lasswell, a political scientist who has done pioneering research in mass communications, once noted three major activities of communication specialists: (1) surveillance of the environment, (2) correlation of the parts of society in responding to the environment, and (3) transmission of the social heritage from one generation to the next.[4] Using Lasswell's categories with some modification and adding a fourth, entertainment, we have a classification of the major aims of communication with which we are concerned.

Surveillance refers to the collection and distribution of information concerning events in the environment, both outside and within any particular society. To some extent it corresponds to what is popularly conceived as the handling of *news*. Acts of correlation, here, include interpretation of information about the environment and prescription for conduct in reaction to these events. In part this activity is popularly identified as *editorial* or *propaganda*. Transmission of culture focuses on the communicating of information, values, and social norms from one generation to another or from members of a group to newcomers. Commonly it is identified as *educational* activity. Finally, *entertainment* refers to communicative acts primarily intended for amusement irrespective of any instrumental effects they might have.

At this point the reader might properly ask: what has become of the focus on *mass* communications? Surely the four activities listed above were carried on long before the invention of modern mass media. This observation is not only correct, but serves to bring into focus precisely the question to be raised here—what are the consequences of performing each of these four activities *by means of mass communication?* For example, what are the consequences of conducting surveillance through the process of mass communications instead of through some alternative system, such as a private intelligence network? That is, what are the results of treating information about events in the environment as items of news to be distributed indiscriminately, simultaneously, and publicly to a large, heterogeneous, anonymous population? Similarly, what are the effects of handling interpretation, cultural transmission, and entertainment as mass communications activities?

The consequences of regularized social activity have long attracted the attention of social scientists concerned with a branch of theory known as functional analysis.[5] Some of the concepts developed by these theoreticians are highly useful for the present discussion.

One of the contemporary contributors to functional theory, Robert K. Merton, distinguishes between the consequences (functions) of a social activity and the aims or purposes behind the activity.[6] Clearly they need not be identical. A local public health campaign may be carried on for the purpose of persuading people to come to a clinic for a check-up. While pursuing this goal, the campaign may have the unanticipated result of improving the morale of the local public health employees, whose everyday work has suddenly been given public attention.[7] Merton terms consequences that are intended *manifest functions* and those that are unintended *latent functions*. He also points out that not every consequence of an activity has positive value for the social system in which it occurs, or for the groups or individuals involved. Consequences that are undesirable from the point of view of the welfare of the society or its members are called *dysfunctions*. Any single act may have both functional and dysfunctional effects. The public health campaign, for instance, might also have frightened some people so much that they failed to report for a check-up lest they find some incurable ailment. Thus the campaign would have been functional insofar as it boosted employee morale and, presumably, efficiency; but it would have been dysfunctional insofar as it had the "boomerang" effect of frightening away potential patients.

Let us now speculate about some possible functions and dysfunctions of handling our communications activities (surveillance, interpretation and prescription, education, and entertainment) as mass communications. Admittedly the account will raise more questions than it answers. But it will also provide a framework within which the role of mass communications in our society may profitably be viewed.

SURVEILLANCE BY MASS MEDIA   Consider what it means to society, and to its individual members, to have available a constant flow of data on events occurring within the society and in the larger world. At the level of the total society, two positive consequences of surveillance are, first, that it often provides *warnings* about imminent threats and dangers in the world—about, say, impending danger from hurricanes or from military attack. Forewarned, the population can mobilize and avert destruction. Second, a flow of data about the environment is *instrumental* to such everyday institutional activities of the society as the stock market, navigation, and air traffic.

For individual members of the society several functions of surveillance can be discerned. First, insofar as personal welfare is linked to social welfare, the warning and instrumental functions of news serve the individual while they serve the society. In addition, several more personal forms of *utility* can be identified. In 1945 a group of social scientists took advantage of a local newspaper strike in New York City to study what people "missed" when they did not receive their regular newspaper. One clearly identifiable function of the newspaper for these urbanites was as a source of information about routine events—providing data on local radio and motion picture performances, sales by local merchants, embarkations, deaths, and the latest fashions. When people "missed" their daily papers they were, in fact, missing a tool for daily living.[8] Another function of mass communicated news is to bestow *prestige*

upon the individuals who make the effort to keep themselves informed about events. That is, making news available to all need not mean that everyone keeps up with it.
To the extent that being informed is considered important
by the society, people who conform to this norm enhance
their prestige within the group. Often those individuals
who select *local* news as their focus of attention emerge
as local opinion leaders in their community, while people
who turn attention to events in the greater society operate
as *cosmopolitan* influentials.[9]

Two sociologists, Paul Lazarsfeld and Robert Merton,
suggest two other functions of mass communications,
which seem to be especially applicable to mass communicated news.[10] These are *status conferral* and the enforcement of social norms (*ethicizing*). Status conferral means
that news reports about a member of any society enhance
his prestige. By focusing the power of the mass media upon
him society confers upon him a high public status. Hence
the premium placed upon publicity and public relations in
modern society. Mass communication has an ethicizing function when it strengthens social control over the individual
members of the mass society by bringing deviant behavior
into public view. Newspaper crusades, for example,
publicize information on norm violation. Such facts might
already have been known privately by many members of
the society; but their disclosure through mass communication creates the social conditions under which most
people must condemn the violations and support public,
rather than private, standards of morality. By this process,
mass communicated news strengthens social control in
large urbanized societies where urban anomymity has
weakened informal face-to-face detection and control of
deviant behavior.

Surveillance through mass communications can prove
dysfunctional as well as functional for society and its
members. First, uncensored news about the world potentially *threatens* the structure of any society. For example,
information about conditions and ideologies in other
societies might lead to invidious comparisons with condi-

tions at home, and hence to pressures toward change. Second, uninterpreted warnings about danger in the environment sometimes lead to *panic* by the mass audience. Thus, in the frequently cited Orson Welles broadcast of an Invasion from Mars, the belief that the radio story was actually a news report contributed to the panic reaction of many listeners.[11]

Dysfunctions can be identified on the individual level too. First, data about dangers in the environment, instead of having a warning function, can heighten *anxieties* within the audience. "War nerves" are an example. Second, too much news can result in *privatization;* the individual, overwhelmed by the data brought to his attention, reacts by turning to matters in his private life, over which he has greater control.[12] Third, access to mass communicated news sometimes causes apathy; having information about the world gives the individual a false sense of mastery over his environment. He spends so much time absorbing news that he takes little direct action; he may believe that to be an informed citizen is equivalent to being an active citizen. Lazarsfeld and Merton have applied to this dysfunctional aspect of mass communications the colorful label of *narcotization.*

INTERPRETATION AND PRESCRIPTION BY MASS MEDIA   The chief function of interpretation and prescription is to prevent such undesirable consequences of the mass communication of news as were noted in the preceding section. The selection, evaluation, and interpretation of news—focusing on what is most important in the environment—tend to prevent over-stimulation and over-mobilization of the population. Most people are fully aware of the economy to them, in time and effort, of editorial activity. For example, in the previously cited study of what missing the newspaper meant to its readers, interviews revealed that people not only missed news about public events but also the evaluation and interpretation of these events which the papers ordinarily provided. Similarly, modern journalists have modified the early twentieth century emphasis on objective reporting of "facts." Many journalists now extend the definition of their occupational role to include the responsibility to evaluate and interpret events for the reader, as by placing them within the larger historical and social context, and evaluating the various sources from which the "facts" emerged.[13]

Like surveillance, the activities of news interpretation and prescription for behavior, when performed as mass communications, can also be dysfunctional. On the level of the total society, such activities can operate to impede social change and enhance conformism insofar as the *public* nature of the communication limits its usefulness for social criticism. That is, since any interpretation critical of the existing social order is readily visible when conducted as a mass communications activity, it can be subjected to whatever preventive sanctions exist within the society. The sanctions need not be connected with official censorship or governmental agencies. They may be economic or unofficial, as in the case of a consumer boycott against a sponsor of a television program criticizing the status quo. When everyone can monitor a communication, discretion generally diverts the content from controversial topics and social criticism. Insofar as useful social change might stem from such criticism, the limitations on editorial activity via mass media prove dysfunctional for the society.

For the individual, these activities are dysfunctional if the interpretation and editing of news by mass media weakens his own critical faculties. When news is edited for him, the individual does not have to sift and sort, interpret and evaluate, information for himself. He is free to accept or reject prefabricated views about the world around him, as presented by the mass media. But at some point, it can be argued, the consumer of predigested ideas, opinions, and views becomes an ineffectual citizen, less capable of functioning as a rational man.

TRANSMISSION OF CULTURE; ENTERTAINMENT   A full analysis of the other two communication activities—transmission of culture (*socialization*) and entertainment—is not practicable here. Several important aspects of these activities will be treated in detail throughout the Study, especially in Chapters 4 and 5. At this point we simply raise a few questions according to the pattern of functional analysis that has been laid out in the preceding sections.

Consider what it means, for example, to society and to its individual members, to have many of the socialization activities (that is, the passing of culture down to the children) handled as mass communications. To what extent does this practice unify the society by giving it a broader base of common norms, values, collective experiences shared by its members? Or, to what extent does a loss of subcultural variety and creativity result from the transmission of a standardized view of culture? One disadvantage for the individual, it may be argued, is that the mass media depersonalize the process of socialization. David Riesman notes that the moral lessons of tales told by mass media cannot be tailored to fit the capacity of the individual listener, as they might have been in face-to-face storytelling. Hence the oversensitive child might make unduly harsh demands upon himself as he internalizes the unmediated cultural lessons from books, films, television, and other mass media.[14] Other questions about the role of mass communication in socialization are discussed in Chapter 5.

Consider, too, the functions and dysfunctions of mass entertainment, in contrast to individualistic, familial, or other private forms of amusement. For example, critics of popular culture argue that mass entertainment is dysfunctional insofar as it fails to raise public taste to the level that might be obtained by such less extensive forms of entertainment as the theater, books, or opera. At the same time, it is argued, there is a loss of quality even in the artistic materials which are mass communicated, as illustrated by a shift in emphasis from form to melody in classical music when it is broadcast.[15] This is not the place, however, to evaluate such claims about popular or mass culture.

This chapter has raised some important questions about

the potential functions and dysfunctions of mass communication in general. Our discussion now turns to alternative organizations of mass communication which have been developed in different societies, so that the reader may gain broader perspective on the American systems.

2

Alternative Systems of Mass Communications: Selected Case Studies

Four Concepts of Mass Media

Three experts on international mass communications have recently found it convenient to view the communications systems of the world as operating—more or less precisely —under four major theories: (1) Soviet-Communist; (2) Libertarian; (3) Social Responsibility; and (4) Authoritarian.[1] Under the first theory may be grouped most of the communications systems of Communist countries, including the Soviet Union itself. Here the mass media— press, radio, film, etc.—have clear and explicit mandates as to their primary objectives. Above all they are committed to carrying Communist theory and policy to the masses, rallying support for the Party and government, and raising the general cultural level of the people. To achieve these aims the Party and government exercise relatively strict control over the media and their operation. The Libertarian theory dominates the Anglo-American and many other Western countries. Emphasis is upon the freedom of the media, especially from government control, although occasionally government regulation, restriction, and operation may be found. Also in the Anglo-American tradition is the third theory which places more emphasis upon the moral and social responsibilities of persons or institutions who operate the mass media. These responsibilities include, for example, obligation to provide the public with information and discussion on important social issues, and avoidance of activities harmful to the public welfare. Often the mass media in Western countries seem to operate under a mixture of these two philosophies, although some writers contend that there is a trend toward the Social Responsibility concept. The last philosophy, the Authoritarian, was characteristic of the earlier European situation and is still current in some countries, often in the less industrialized areas, such as the Middle East. Under this theory the media —private or public—are clearly subordinate to the state and are restrained from major criticisms of the government or its officials or both. Such restraint may be achieved through a variety of methods, such as relatively strict governmental procedures of licensing and censorship.

In this chapter we examine several differing systems of mass communication. Examples will be drawn mainly from the field of broadcasting, occasionally from other media. We consider first the Soviet system; then, briefly, the British, Canadian, and American; and finally selected characteristics of communication in non-industrial countries, especially the Middle East.

A word of warning—our purpose is not to judge one communication system as better or more desirable than another, for such personal judgment violates scientific reporting. From the perspective of functional analysis, however, the reader may discover that some of the organizational features described appear to be useful for the maintenance of the social systems within which they operate; others, and even the same features, may appear dysfunctional for the society and its citizens. We can make no overall evaluation here of the net balance of functional and dysfunctional elements of each communications system, for such a task is beyond the objectives and resources of this Study. Our approach in this chapter is primarily descriptive and occasionally analytical. We hope that comparative information about a variety of communications systems will provide the reader with a broader framework within which he can view and understand the more familiar American forms of mass communications.

Case #1: The Soviet-Communist System

Of all the mass communications systems in the world, the most intriguing for the American reader, because it contrasts so sharply with his own, probably is the Soviet-Communist. The major outlines of this system have been analyzed by Alex Inkeles, a sociologist associated with the Russian Research Center at Harvard University, in *Public Opinion in Soviet Russia*.[2] This scholarly work provides the major source of the information reported in the following sections.

BROADCASTING   The Soviet medium that presents perhaps the most dramatic contrast with the American form is the broadcasting system. Description of this system best begins with the unit closest to the citizen: the radio receiver. In 1955 there were approximately 26 million radio receivers in the U.S.S.R., or about one for every eight persons.[3] (In the United States in 1954 there were approximately 127 million radio receivers, or nearly one for every person.[4]) Less than one fifth of these receivers, however, resemble radio familiar to Americans: sets capable of receiving broadcasts directly from the air.[5] Most consist of *wired* receiving sets, comparable to loud-speakers, which can be turned on or off but cannot be tuned to receive any broadcast except that distributed over a network of wired speakers called a radio-diffusion exchange. The radio-diffusion exchange operates a regular receiver which picks up a broadcast in the same manner as the American's radio set, and then sends it over wires to the loud-speakers (wired sets) of its subscribers. Often either the wired sets or public address systems are located in public places—recreation halls, factory shops, collective farms, reading rooms—where radio listening then becomes a group experience. In such settings it is possible for local representatives of the Communist Party to "agitate" the audience by interpreting and commenting upon the broadcast and by leading group discussions.

Each radio-diffusion exchange is part of the lower level of Soviet broadcasting. There are two other levels: the local and the central. Under special conditions the diffusion exchange may originate its own programs, but for the most part its service consists of distributing, over wires to its subscribers, the programs broadcast by the local and central stations. Local broadcasting refers to the network of regional stations which supply the several territories and republics of the Soviet Union. Unlike the lower exchanges, local stations often create their own programs. For a sizeable part of their broadcast time, however, they function as part of zonal or national networks, usually rebroadcasting programs originating at the central broadcasting level. Central broadcasting comes from Moscow. It consists primarily of all-union programs—broadcasts directed to all citizens in the Soviet—plus special programs for selected audiences, outlying areas, etc. These three levels of broadcasting—central, local and lower—provide a network of radio service transmitting in seventy languages and reaching citizens scattered over a country covering more than 8 million square miles.

How is this vast network controlled? For each of the three organizational levels of broadcasting there corresponds a system of radio committees, responsible to a central All-Union Radio Committee. Generally this committee is or, at least, was, responsible for "the organization, planning, and operational direction of all radiobroadcasting in the U.S.S.R., including radio diffusion by lower radiobroadcasting exchanges in district centers, Machine-Tractor Stations, and so forth." [6] Within this All-Union Committee there are several units, one of which—the Administration of Central Broadcasting—"plans, organizes, and executes the programs broadcast by stations directly under the operational control of the Radio Committee." [7] This refers to the all-union and special broadcasts for outlying regions, usually originating in the Moscow stations. Another unit of the All-Union Radio Committee is the Administration of Local Broadcasting, which supervises the broadcasting by local radio committees and by the directors of radio diffusion exchanges. For local broadcasting, that is, within the various republics, territories, regions, and larger cities, there are local radio committees responsible for rebroadcasting the central programs and planning and broadcasting their own programs. These local radio committees are defined as the "local organs" of the All-Union Committee, and their chairmen are "representatives" or "authorized agents" of that Committee.[8] Most of these local committees include a department of lower broadcasting, which exercises control over the work of the radio-diffusion exchanges in their own area. The radio-diffusion exchanges generally are managed by "editors," but some (usually those exchanges permitted to originate their own programs) operate under the direction of "editorial boards." Both the editors and editorial boards are under the ultimate authority of the All-Union Radio Committee. The actual operation of the exchanges, however, may be an enterprise of such public agencies as the Ministry of Communications, All-Union Central Committee of Trade Unions, Ministry of Agriculture and Ministry of State Farms, municipal authorities or other local organizations. In this way, the overall structure of radio broadcasting is highly centralized, with maximum authority located in the All-Union Radio Committee, lesser authority and responsibility held by the various local committees, and least authority exercised by the diffusion exchanges which supply the local listener.

Inkeles reports that this broadcasting system is effectively controlled by the Communist Party through a combination of indirect and direct mechanisms. Consider, for example, the Party's three chief methods of guiding the central Radio Committee. First, the Party issues decisions criticizing the work of the committee and directing its future activity. Such directives are customarily issued by the Party's Central Committee, through its Department of Propaganda and Agitation. Second, the Party places trusted officials in positions of responsibility and control on the Radio Committee. Third, the rank-and-file employees of the communications system include a large number of Party members, who can see that the Radio Committee operates in line with the Party's directives and who are expected to report any deviations to their Party cells. On the local and lower levels of broadcasting similar controls exist—thus the local radio committees are supervised by local Party organizations, and the "editors" of lower radio-diffusion exchanges are supervised by such local Party organs as local trade union committees.

How did the Soviet wired diffusion arrangement come about? And, once established, what are its functions and dysfunctions for Soviet society? Inkeles summarizes four arguments commonly given in support of the system[9] that also provide clues as to its origin and current functions. Initially the system provided an economical solution to communication over a large land area to a population with limited financial and technical resources. For example, a simple wired speaker cost less than one-tenth the amount of a regular receiver to install and to operate; in addition the supply of parts required was obviously much less. At the same time, the wired system provided higher quality reception than regular sets because the single lower-level receiver that serves many wired speakers was of higher quality than the usual private set. Third, it is argued that the wired network facilitates local communications and permits such communication to continue without enemy detection during war. Finally, the restriction of the listener to one program, or at best a few programs, offered by his set enhances the control and propagandistic power of the system, virtually eliminating the reception of outside propaganda.

The major features of the Soviet system—wired speakers in radio-diffusion exchanges, levels of broadcasting, collective listening, public address systems—may be regarded as products of the natural history of broadcasting in that society. That is, they represent one functional organizational pattern (not necessarily the only possible pattern) developed historically to meet the particular technical, economic, social, and political conditions of the moment: "the great distances to be covered in the Soviet Union, the limited number of broadcasting stations available, and the difficulties of producing a sufficient number of regular sets to meet the needs of the population." [10] Furthermore, the pattern is highly compatible with the social and political ideology that directs all mass communication in the Soviet, to aid the Communist Party in its Bolshevic education of the masses, a concept of leadership early emphasized by Lenin. According to Leninist philosophy, the Party has, among other objectives, the clear duty to lead the proletariat, raising their general cultural level, and guiding them toward their social, economic, and political destiny. Under this philosophy, the radio and other mass media are regarded primarily as instruments for achieving the Party's goals.[11]

SOVIET PRESS   No newspapers in the Soviet Union are privately owned. They are published by the Communist Party, the government, or such public associations as trade union organizations, sports clubs, youth organizations, factory groups, and collective farms.[12] In general, the press consists of papers published at various "levels" corresponding to the major administrative-territorial divisions within the Soviet Union, and specialized along a number of functional lines. Geographically, the levels of the press include: the central all-union press, which circulates throughout the Soviet Union; the provincial press, including the republican, territorial, and regional papers; the local press, including the district, city, and lower (primary) press; and single-copy typewritten or handwritten "wall" newspapers tacked on bulletin boards in factories, farm buildings, and the like. The number of papers published on each level increases from the all-union papers (about 25 published, with an estimated circulation of about 7.5 million), through the provincial sector (about 460 papers with over 10 million circulation), the local sector (about 6700 papers with over 13 million circulation), to the several hundred thousand wall newspapers.

Each sector of the press has special roles. Thus the all-union press carries the message of the central authorities, publishes the Party line, and generally is the pattern and main source of material for all newspapers of similar functional type in provincial and local sectors. The provincial press translates these materials for a particular region, clarifies and discusses regional economic and political problems, and propagandizes for the Party. The local press is charged with teaching the masses and translating Party directives into daily life, but cannot discuss Party theory or other top-level matters.

Within each of the three main sectors of the Soviet Press there are papers of differing functional type, specially designed to treat a particular subject matter or to reach special audiences. For example, there are the official Communist Party publications—*Pravda* at the central level, *Soviet Ukraine* at the provincial level. *Izvestiya* of the Supreme Soviets and *Red Star* and *Red Fleet* of the military services, are examples of all-union government publications. Papers written for workers have ranged, at times, from *Trud,* the publication of the All-Union Trade Union Council, to local papers such as the *Subway Shockworker* and *Autoplant Workers.*

Each level of the press is ultimately subject to the direction, inspection, and control of the Central Committee of the All-Union Communist Party, which also confirms the appointment of editors. The Central Committee exercises its control through its Department of Propaganda and Agitation, which contains sectors responsible for the central, provincial, and local presses. Each level is also subject to control by the press sector of the propaganda and agitation department of the Communist Party committee that operates on that level of administration. This sector nominates the editors for its level, for example, supervises the press in that area, and reviews and criticizes the press on the next lower level. Thus a Republican Party committee's press sector would nominate the editor in that Republic and supervise the press there, while reviewing and criticizing the district or city papers in its area. Each lower committee of the Communist Party is, of course, ultimately responsible to the Central Committee. Each paper is also subject to review and criticism: the lower press may be criticized by the district paper, the district by the regional, the regional by the central all-union paper. Finally, cutting across all levels of the press is the potential power of the chief official agency of censorship, *Glavlit*. It seems, however, that *Glavlit* actually exercises little power since it cannot censor much of the content of Party and government publications. Hence, in a system controlled by so many other means, direct censorship seems to play a minor role.

SOVIET FILM   Formal responsibility for the movie industry rests with the Ministry of Education, but the Communist Party effects day-to-day direction, review, and control of this medium by a variety of methods similar to those described above. Basically, the film is seen as another medium for propaganda, agitation, and cultural elevation of the masses. More important than this conception of the film's role, from our perspective, are several facts about the facilities for exhibition of films in the Soviet.

Though there are approximately 40,000 cinemas in the Soviet Union, over 80 per cent of these are in villages. Furthermore, a large number of the urban movies are exhibited in clubs and schools. Finally, about half of the 50,000 or 60,000 projectors in the U.S.S.R. operate in mobile units. These facts point to two important features of the Soviet film industry—first, the dominance of small group audience situations over the larger (potentially anonymous) audience situations; and second, the wide distribution of equipment designed to extend the cinema to a large, otherwise inaccessible audience.[13]

SUMMARY   The Soviet system of mass communications, as the preceding description brings out, emphasizes the following characteristics: (1) It is a *planned* system, both in its formal organization and communication content. Newspapers, radio transmitters, diffusion networks, and film studios can be altered to fit the changing needs of their society—expanding or contracting, focusing on a special segment of the audience, and so on. (2) The media are operated under a philosophy strongly committed to the *Communist Party line* and the achievement of Soviet goals. (3) Soviet communications involve a high degree of *review and control* of communications content. (4) There is a high degree of *specialization*, especially with respect to the level or type of audience toward whom each medium is directed. For example, special programs may be directed only toward those farmers who are linked by a particular radio-diffusion network of wired receivers; or separate newspapers may each specialize for labor, farm or youth readers. (5) The arrangement of the Soviet media maximizes opportunities for audience exposure in *group situations*, listening to the radio in public halls, reading news while gathered before the wall newspapers, watching movies projected by rural mobile units, visiting peasant reading huts.

At the risk of oversimplification, the four communications activities which concerned us earlier may be ranked as follows. (1) The Soviet system gives priority to the interpretation of events and to prescriptions for conduct for the audience. For example, the concept of "news" in the Soviet press does not mean the rapid reporting of current events. Rather, the Soviet editor is responsible for *selecting* from the events of past and recent history those incidents which illustrate or document the ongoing social processes, especially the process of Socialist construction. And a large portion of the daily press is often devoted to suggestions, instructions (in short, prescriptions) for the conduct of local Party officials, workers, and others. (2) High priority is also given to the transmission of Soviet culture, including not only culture in the broader sense of the basic values and norms of the civilization but also artistic and intellectual materials. Thus, over half of the broadcasts consist of music, most of it classical. (3) Entertainment receives less emphasis, except for those forms of entertainment which show maximum promise of improving the audience's taste, or of contributing to its political or cultural education. (4) Surveillance or reporting of news events, as we know it, plays little part in the philosophy of the system. The press is not obliged to transmit information about current events to its mass audience, nor to be objective in its reporting. The Soviet system thus presents a striking contrast with the American or other Libertarian systems.

We turn now to two systems of communications determined partially by technical necessities but also by philosophies quite different from the Soviet Russian, namely, the British and Canadian. Our discussion is limited to broadcasting, the structure of which has been analyzed by Charles Siepmann in his work on *Radio, Television, and Society,* upon which the following section draws.[14]

Case #2: British and Canadian Broadcasting

Broadcasting in Britain operates as a monopoly granted by a Royal Charter to the British Broadcasting Corporation. As a public corporation, the BBC has certain obligations to the government (for example, any government department may demand that the BBC transmit information considered important to the public), but it is neither controlled nor operated by any branch of the government. Formally, the BBC is headed by a Board of Governors, appointed by the Queen through her Prime Minister, and is operated under a Director General and a professional staff who are employees of the Board of Governors rather than political appointees. Operations are financed in part by licensing radio owners and in part through revenues from the *Radio Times,* a weekly program guide. Fifty-seven transmitters supply the British with three types of programs, each on its own frequency. the "Light" programs, the "Home" services—both offered nationwide—and the "Third" program which reaches about 50 per cent of Britain's population. In addition, six regional stations (in Scotland, Wales, North Ireland, northern, middle, and western England) may substitute their own programs for some of the Home programs.

Technical limitations have played a considerable part

in the natural history of broadcasting in Britain. Because of proximity to the continent, the British early had to reach an international agreement concerning the broadcast frequencies they alone could use without interference. As a result, Britain was limited to only two broadcast frequencies with power sufficient to cover the entire nation. The license to use these two airways therefore became a matter of vital political, social, and economic consequence, and it was decided that both frequencies should be entrusted to a public corporation rather than being placed in private hands (as, indeed, earlier British broadcasting had been).

But technical limitations alone cannot account for the unique system of British broadcasting. This system also has been influenced by an ideological commitment made early in the history of broadcasting in Britain, under which radio was regarded as an opportunity for the cultural improvement of a mass audience. From its vantage position of monopolistic control, the BBC was committed to a program policy designed to facilitate the cultural enlightenment of the average listener. Each of the BBC's three sets of programs—Light, Home, and Third—represented a level in a hierarchy of cultural quality. Listeners initially attracted to the entertainment provided by the Light program were, in time, to be weaned from these offerings to the more serious material of the Home programs, and ultimately their taste could be cultivated so as to lead them to the literary, musical, and artistic fineries of the Third program. Furthermore, as time went on, it was planned to have each of the three programs also raise its standards: the Light program of any year would be less frivolous than that of years past, and so on. BBC's monopolistic control over programs promised to contribute to the realization of this educational goal. Hence technical imperatives and ideological objectives went hand-in-hand in determining the current form of broadcasting in Britain.

Our purpose here is not to evaluate the relative success or failure of the British program policy. However, a brief review of some of its alleged advantages and disadvantages

will provide clues to certain of the functional and dysfunctional aspects of the arrangement. Several of these arguments object to the monopolistic character of BBC; others
refer to the paternalistic philosophy of the three-level
programming; still others criticize the specific content of
one or more of the programs—as the following objections
illustrate.[15]

(1) A monopoly of broadcasting alone is not sufficient
for the achievement of the goals of the BBC. It is argued
that a monopoly of only one segment of mass communications is inefficient because the audience can "es-
cape" from broadcasting to lighter entertainment provided by film, books, or other media. Furthermore,
cultural education requires a long period of socialization,
as provided possibly by university life, and support for
higher taste within the home and peer group surround-
ings.

(2) Monopoly is not necessary for the achievement of
BBC objectives. Rather, what is needed is the guarantee
of high quality broadcasts being available for listeners
whose tastes have been cultivated so that they can listen
to good material and shun the inferior.

(3) Monopoly creates sluggishness and inefficiency.
(Siepmann argues, however, that the history of innova-
tions within BBC indicates that this objection is without
foundation in this instance.)

(4) Monopoly tends to a self-perpetuation of the organization, secrecy surrounding its operations, and the
like.

(5) Monopoly sometimes prevents radio from providing
necessary or desirable materials. For example, for many
years the BBC avoided broadcasts by named news
analysts or debates about current legislative controversies
in Parliament because it was felt that the monopolistic
position of BBC might give undue power to such broadcasts.

(6) The "high culture" offered as the fare for those

whose tastes develop according to the BBC plan is questioned. Critics argue that the content of the Third Program reflects a nostalgic culture of an intellectual aristocracy educated in the Oxford or Cambridge tradition—a concept more suited to the eighteenth than the twentieth century. Hence, it is argued, the program places too much emphasis on the fine arts and culture and too little on those subjects vital to present-day survival, for example, science.

Television broadcasting, like radio, was a BBC monopoly until 1954, when the government approved the creation of the Independent Television Authority. The ITA began telecasting in competition with BBC in 1955. Programs for the ITA are provided by privately financed program contractors who sell advertising.

It is too soon to evaluate fully the impact of commercial television upon either BBC radio or television audiences. BBC continues to provide television service for the greatest number of British viewers; but research evidence indicates that commercial television is attracting a sizeable proportion of the viewers in areas where a choice between BBC and ITA is possible.[16] What the distribution of the viewing audience will be, once the novelty of commercial television is past, cannot be predicted. Nor can we forecast the impact of commercial television upon the BBC's broad cultural "experiment" in elevating public taste. Comparative content analyses of BBC and ITA television programming, however, indicate that the BBC devotes a considerably higher proportion of its television time to programs of an informational or orientation type.[17]

Canadian radio and television broadcasting, like the British, is a mixture of private and public operations. Again, the process through which this system developed has been influenced by both technical and ideological considerations. On the technical side, the Canadians faced a problem similar to Soviet Russia's, that of providing coverage over a vast territory with relatively limited facilities. On the ideological side, the Canadian government was concerned with developing and maintaining a Canadian culture which would not be overridden by the United States (whose radio stations blanketed the Canadian border, where about 80 per cent of the Canadian population lived) and which would provide broadcasts to suit the tastes of minority groups as well as the majority of Canadian listeners.[18]

After extensive legislative debate during the 1920s and 1930s, the Canadian Broadcasting Corporation was established in 1936. It was organized as a public corporation (similar to BBC), responsible to a Board of Governors, and financed by revenue from licenses on receivers and from its network and station operation. In order to extend radio coverage to outlying local areas of the Dominion, the CBC permitted privately owned stations to operate, using them as affiliated outlets for its network stations as well as sources for original local broadcasts. A similar policy was followed in the case of television.[19]

In addition to its network and station operations, the CBC serves as the official regulatory agency for broadcasting in Canada, recommending licenses for the private stations, regulating their broadcasts, and so on. By clearly subordinating private stations to the CBC, this arrangement, according to supporters, helps to achieve the national goal of maintaining Canadian culture and supplying programs for minorities. Stations are thus prevented from disregarding the CBC network programs and from carrying so many network shows from the United States as to permit the cultural invasion of Canada.

Case #3: The American Broadcasting System

No other country in the world today has as much mass communication as the United States. Each day, for example, over 55 million newspapers are circulated—about one copy for every three people. Over 127 million radios are available—almost one per person. At least 35 million television sets are in American homes—about one for every five viewers. And millions of magazines and comic books circulate every month.*

For the most part, the American media are privately owned and operate as profit-making organizations. But they are subject to some government regulation, especially when their operations require the use of the public domain or touch upon matters of public welfare. Hence radio and television broadcasting, which make use of public airways, require a license from the government; laws prohibit the transmission of material considered libelous; censorship has been employed in time of war; and so on. Aside from such specific situational regulations, however, the American media operate essentially under a philosophy of minimum (and if possible no) government restrictions.

The legal roots of the American approach towards mass communication can be found in the First Amendment to the Constitution, which guarantees freedom of speech and press. Each of the mass media at various times in its history has defended itself from excessive government control by recourse to this amendment. This legal protection of the media has had substantial support from American public opinion. For example, national polls have shown that at least 95 per cent of the public say that they believe in freedom of speech.[20]

Nevertheless, neither the law nor public opinion endorses *unlimited* freedom of expression. The Courts have held that freedom of the press does not extend to the publication of obscene materials or topics that constitute a clear and present danger to the nation. Public sentiment likewise qualifies its approval of freedom. Thus national surveys conducted by *Fortune* magazine during the 1930s show that only about half of the public thought that newspapers should be allowed to print anything they choose

* *World Communications: Press, Radio, Film, Television* (Paris: Unesco, 1956), pp. 118-122. The figures are taken for about 1954 and no doubt under-represent the current situation. They are used here, however, because their date makes them comparable with statistics reported for other countries at that time.

except libelous matter. Topics which many people at that
time felt should not be allowed in newspapers and magazines include divorce hearings, paintings of nudes, and
attacks on public officials.[21]

Despite these qualifications, the basic American commitment to minimum governmental intervention is evident
even among those people who would restrict the press.
When asked by what method newspapers and magazines
should be prevented from writing about the undesirable
topics only 8 per cent of the critics advocated government
control of the press, and less than 1 per cent wanted a
board of censors. The most frequently mentioned method
was "public opinion," the next most frequent the "editor's
good taste." A similar preference for self-regulation by
the industry instead of increased government control was
expressed by persons most critical of American radio during a national survey of radio listening in 1947.[22]

The following sections examine, very briefly, the current
organization of broadcasting in America, touching on the
changing role of the government and some of the historical
steps in the development of the present organizational
structure.[23]

CURRENT STRUCTURE OF THE RADIO AND TELEVISION IN-
DUSTRY   Anyone intending to transmit radio or television
signals within the United States must first obtain the permission of the federal government through the Federal
Communications Commission. The FCC is empowered to
issue, review, and renew licenses for broadcasting, which
stipulate the frequency on which the broadcaster must
remain, the power and times of his transmission, and other
terms of operation.

Since technical conditions limit the number of frequencies available for radio or television broadcasting, not
every applicant can obtain a license. Some criteria of
priority had to be developed, and a certain amount of
sharing of frequencies is necessary to maximize the service
provided by the available frequencies. Some radio stations
can operate during certain hours of the day only, for

example, when there is little chance that their signals will interfere with those of other nearby or distant stations. Other stations are given priority to operate with stronger signals and at different times in order to reach parts of the country which might not otherwise be serviced. Maximizing the public service performed by radio and television broadcasting is a major concern of the federal government. Hence each applicant for a license or renewal must demonstrate that he will meet a public need and provide a public service if permitted to operate.

Because of these technical problems, broadcasting has been subject to more direct regulation by the national government than most of the other American media. Still this control tends to be more regulatory than restrictive in its intent and effects. Llewellyn White, in his excellent history of American radio,[24] identifies the following periods in the history of government regulation of radio broadcasting:

(1) the laissez-faire period, 1922-1927
(2) the traffic-control period, 1927-1932
(3) the cleanup period, 1932-1937
(4) the trust-busting period, 1937-1944
(5) the public-service era, from 1944 on.

Radio during the early years was controlled under the old Radio Act of 1912, which empowered the Secretary of Commerce to issue licenses specifying frequency of operation. Prior to 1922, licensees were primarily maritime stations and a few amateurs, but when broadcasting "arrived" the number of applicants increased greatly. The courts held that the Secretary of Commerce was required to issue licenses and to assign frequencies to all applicants. But as the transmitters increased in number, they began to interfere with one another—some stations drifted from their assigned frequencies, more powerful stations blanked out weaker ones, and portable transmitters added to the confusion. Hopes for self-regulation within the industry were not realized and members of the industry began to look to the federal government for relief from the traffic congestion on the airways. In 1927 a new Radio Act was legislated, asserting the federal government's right to regulate all forms of radio communication within the United States through a system of licensing to be administered by a Federal Radio Commission. (This authority became the Federal Communications Commission under a new Communications Act of 1934.)

White uses the relative emphases that this Commission gave to various types of government regulation to identify the four historical periods that followed the initial era of laissez-faire, and to illustrate the growing demand for greater social responsibility, culminating in the public service era.[25] And most of the major governmental decisions concerning television have been made during this latter era.

The government's concern for responsible broadcasting has been paralleled by movements within the industry itself toward greater self-regulation and the assumption of its public service obligations, as demonstrated in the codes of ethics for radio and television adopted by the National Association of Broadcasters and later by the National Association of Radio and Television Broadcasters. These codes not only assert the freedom of the broadcaster but also underscore his responsibility to the public.[26] Enforcement of both federal and self-imposed norms in broadcasting is complicated, however, by the structure of the industry, which sometimes assigns the power of program construction not only to the individual station owner-operator but also to networks or to advertising agencies.

Each radio or television station is responsible for selecting the material that it broadcasts. Some of this the station originates, but many stations also carry programs distributed through one or another of the regional or national networks with which a station becomes affiliated. The networks own a few important stations of their own (primarily in the major metropolitan centers) but the affiliated stations supply their greatest number of outlets. An affiliated station agrees to put aside certain broadcast hours for carrying network programs. In turn the network supplies

the programming for these hours and sells the local station's time on the national market. Both the network and
local stations share in the profits; in addition the local
station may make other hours available to the network
in return for the programming supplied. The "network"
of stations thus created may, in fact, vary from time to
time and from program to program as each of the potential
members of the chain agrees to "hook-in" or not. Networks
need no license, except for the stations they own and
operate themselves. But networks have provided important
support for codes of self-regulation within the industry.

Money for most stations comes through the sale of time
to advertisers. On the local level a potential sponsor may
deal directly with the station. On the national level, however, most advertisers deal with the networks through one
or another of the advertising agencies located along Madi-
son Avenue, New York. Either directly or through an
agency, the advertiser may buy time for spot announce-
ments about his product or he may sponsor a particular
program. Some of these programs are created and controlled by the station itself (private or network), some are
created by independent producers, and others are created
by the advertising agencies. During recent years many of
the major nationally distributed radio programs have been
of the third type, over which the network and its stations
have had relatively little control. Since the advertising
agencies are not themselves directly engaged in broadcasting they need no license and are not responsible to the
FCC.[27] Networks, however, have played a more active role
in the production and programming of television shows.

THE SHAPING OF THE AMERICAN SYSTEM   The sociological
history of radio in America, like that of the other mass
media, is complex, only partially known, and hard to
evaluate at this time. Yet certain broad periods, similar to
those discernible in the development of the other media,
can be distinguished in broadcasting.

The initial period in the history of radio may be characterized as one of great amateur inventiveness, experi-

mentation, and unregulated growth. Then, with the promise of commercial advantages, a continuing struggle for power and control of the industry developed. Legal fights over patents on the technical components and processes necessary for radio communication became "patent wars," from which a few large-scale organizations emerged to dominate the industry. In time some of these giants involved combinations either within one branch of the industry (for example, manufacturing), between several branches of the industry (for example, manufacturing and broadcasting), or between several different mass media industries (for example, joint ownership of newspapers and radio). Occasionally communications empires resulted, within which broadcasting was only a part. One such empire is the Radio Corporation of America.[28]

R.C.A. was formed in 1919 to purchase the radio rights and assets of the American Marconi Company (then controlled by British Marconi). At that time commercial radio broadcasting had not yet begun, but it was subsequently developed by several organizations, including R.C.A. Competition became especially keen between American Telephone & Telegraph and R.C.A. Each of these organizations built a network of affiliated stations revolving around their major owned station in the New York area, WEAF and WJZ respectively. In 1926 after an agreement between these two organizations and others, R.C.A. emerged as the major broadcaster. R.C.A. developed commercial broadcasting through a subsidiary organization, the National Broadcasting Company, which was soon reorganized as two semi-independent networks: the Blue Network, centering on the old R.C.A. network of stations affiliated with WJZ, and the Red Network, the stations affiliated with WEAF (which A.T. and T. sold to R.C.A.).

Within a few decades of its founding R.C.A. extended its operations to include many diverse communications activities. For example, it established two subsidiaries to handle the old Marconi business—the Radiomarine Corporation of America and R.C.A. Communications. It obtained control of the Victor Talking Machine Company and a number of other companies, permitting it eventually to expand its manufacturing of radio receivers, phonograph recordings, and electronic parts and equipment, through the R.C.A. Victor Division. Other subsidiaries were developed for servicing electronic equipment (R.C.A. Service), for research (R.C.A. Laboratories), for training (R.C.A. Institute), and for distribution of products (R.C.A. International Division). Hence network broadcasting—the primary function of the National Broadcasting Company—became, in this instance, part of a vast communications organization involved in manufacturing, distribution, sales, service, telecommunications, recording, broadcasting, training, and research.

N.B.C. is not unique. Other national networks (notably Columbia and American) have their share of organizational connections with non-broadcasting activities in the larger world of the radio industry and mass communications, portrayals of which are readily available.[29]

The full story of the social, economic, and political forces that have shaped the structure of American mass media is of course too complex to cover here. Many volumes have appeared during the past decade, treating one or another of the American media. But despite these excellent accounts, the definitive sociological history of these media has never been written. And perhaps none is possible, for it may well be that the detailed data necessary for such analysis are already lost in the unwritten social history of the past half-century.

Case #4:
Communications in Non-Industrial Countries

Today many of the predominantly agricultural, less "developed" countries have a rather limited system of mass communications, often operated under what has been called an "authoritarian" philosophy, which holds that the primary function of the mass media is "to support and advance the policies of the government in power; and to service the state." [30] To this end, the state exercises strong control over the press and other media through censorship, restrictive licenses, and so on, although these media need not be government owned. But criticism of the government and its officials is usually forbidden.

In this section, however, we are not concerned either with the authoritarian philosophy or with the details of media operation and controls. Rather, the discussion centers upon two characteristics of communications systems which are of great significance in non-industrial countries (although they may also be found in industrial nations). These features are, first, the extensiveness of group exposure to the mass media, and, second, the ubiquitous operation of a network of word-of-mouth communications which is often linked to the mass media. To illustrate these two characteristics we draw upon a study of radio audiences in four Arabic countries—Egypt, Jordan, Lebanon, and Syria—conducted by the Bureau of Applied Social Research of Columbia University in 1952.[31] While recent political events in the Middle East may have altered some aspects of the communications system, there is no evidence that either of these two features has changed significantly.

GROUP LISTENING   By Western standards, these four countries have an extremely low ratio of mass media outlets to total population.[32] For example, Egypt, with a population of about 22 million, has a daily newspaper circulation of about 500,000 or 1 copy for every 44 persons. There are 405,000 radio receivers, or about 1 for every 54 persons. (The United States has a daily newspaper circulation of about 1 copy for every 3 persons and nearly one radio set per person.) Figures for the other three countries are comparable: Jordan, with a population of about 1,360,000, has about 14,000 radio receivers, excluding village loudspeakers; Lebanon, population 1,353,000, has 45,000 radio sets; Syria, population 3,535,000, has 50,000 sets. But these figures can be deceptive if taken as measures of the size of radio audiences in the Middle East, for each set services several persons and often, through group listening, a sizeable portion of an entire village.

While most of the radio auditors reported in the Bureau's study listened at home, a sizeable minority (30 per cent) usually did so outside the home—in local coffeehouses, in the homes of friends or neighbors, in schools, clubs, at work, or elsewhere. Auditing outside the home —in group situations—was more likely to be the pattern for the poor and destitute than for the minority of well-to-do citizens:

> This analysis of general radio listening in four Arabic countries has turned up one phenomenon which, by American standards, is uncommon. That is the great amount of listening which goes on outside the home— in coffee houses, in the homes of friends and neighbors, and so on. These guest listeners, who are such by necessity rather than by choice, are the poor and uneducated segments of the population who cannot afford to buy radios. But, despite the difficulties which they have in hearing radio, they are a sustained audience. More than half of them claim to listen almost every day. And large numbers, although not a majority, report that they plan their listening in advance.[33]

WORD-OF-MOUTH COMMUNICATION A second important feature of the Arabic radio audience is the significant role of informal communication. According to the Bureau's study,

> Recent studies of personal influence show how important word of mouth communication is, even in countries where the formal media are well established and widely distributed. It is all the more important in the Middle East where for centuries it has been the major channel of influence and where the newer media, which might supplant it, have not yet been fully developed." [34]

The significance of this pattern is brought out by noting the usual source of news for these Arab radio listeners. In the investigation, 10 per cent reported that they usually relied solely on other persons to provide them with the news; another 25 per cent used both mass media and word-of-mouth communications for their news. Thus, even among persons who were already members of the audience of at least one mass medium—radio—over a third received their news by word-of-mouth. Furthermore, as with group listening to the radio, dependence on word-of-mouth communication was especially prevalent among those persons with the least amount of formal education. For example, of the illiterate radio listeners about a third usually depended solely on word-of-mouth communications for their news in contrast to only 4 per cent of the college educated listeners.

Face-to-face communicators, their role in the flow of information and influence in the society, and their relationship to the mass media are of great sociological significance.[35] We shall study this matter again, in the following chapter, as we examine certain characteristics of mass audiences in the United States.

3

Sociology of the Audience

Is There a Mass Audience?

Mass communication by our own definition, is directed toward audiences that are relatively large and heterogeneous and whose members are anonymous so far as the communicator is concerned. These three audience characteristics help, in part, to distinguish mass communication from other more limited, directed, and personal forms. The term "mass audience" connotes just such qualities of size, heterogeneity, and anonymity. But in its earlier technical and current common usage, "mass audience" also implies something more. It suggests that audiences share many or all of the sociological characteristics of a special type of human collectivity, a *mass*.

What is a mass? One sociologist, Herbert Blumer, isolates four sociological components which, taken together, identify a mass:

First, its membership may come *from all walks of life,* and from all distinguishable social strata; it may include people of different class position, of different vocation, of different cultural attainment, and of different wealth. . . . Second, the mass is an anonymous group, or more exactly, is composed of *anonymous individuals*. Third, there exists *little interaction* or exchange of experience between the members of the mass. They are usually physically separated from one another, and being anonymous, do not have the opportunity to mill as do the members of the crowd. Fourth, the mass is *very loosely organized* and is not able to act with the concertedness or unity that marks the crowd.[1]

The reader will note that this concept of the mass, if applied to audience members, would regard them as not only heterogeneous but also anonymous and isolated from one another. In short, they are like separate atoms which together comprise the mass audience.

Usually accompanying this concept of a mass audience is an image of the communications media as acting directly upon the individual audience members—reaching each member or not, influencing him directly or not. This view of mass communication has been called the "hypodermic needle model"—each audience member being personally and directly "stuck" by the medium's message, along with the rest of the people in the mass audience.[2] Once it has stuck him, the communication may or may not influence him, according to whether or not it is potent enough to "take."

Recently both the concept of a mass audience and the "hypodermic needle model" of the communication process have been subjected to theoretical and empirical challenge. As sociological research developed during the past two decades both concepts were modified along several lines.

For one thing, a conception of the audience has emerged in which greater notice is taken of the social context within which each audience member operates. The individual (although he is anonymous to the communicator) is rarely genuinely anonymous in his social environment. Ordinarily, he is a member of a network of primary and secondary groupings—his family, friendship groups, occupational circles, and so on—which influence his opinions and attitudes. Inevitably, they affect the way in which he is exposed to mass communication, how he interprets or reacts to any specific communication, and the extent to which he will or can modify his behavior in compliance with the message.

Illustrative of the research in this area is the recent work of sociologists John and Matilda Riley involving exploratory experiments on the effect of peer group membership on communications behavior. They found, among other things, that children who were well integrated members of their peer groups had less preference for radio and television shows of action and violence than had other children. They also were more likely to interpret the content of such action programs in terms of their social utility for advancing the play activity of their group than the children who were isolated from peer group interaction. Less integrated children were more likely to prefer these action stories and to dwell upon the literal interpretation of the message (for example, as creepy or scary).[3] Here is one of many examples of the fact that the social pattern within which the audience member is involved clearly affects his selection and response to mass communication.

Research has also revealed that in many instances the members of an audience are—at the very moment of exposure—participating in a group experience. We have already noted this characteristic of audiences in the Soviet Union, where group listening to the radio is quite common. But there are parallels in other societies. For example, going to the movies in the United States is often likely to be a group experience.[4] Again, the non-anonymous, social nature of the situation may affect the audience's response.

Finally, the social connections of the individual provide him with a communication network, on a personal face-to-face basis. This informal network often gives him indirect access to mass communication material which does not reach him directly. There is growing evidence, in fact, to support the hypothesis that mass communications messages do not always reach all members of their ultimate audience directly (hypodermic needle model). Sometimes, through a two-step process, they first reach one layer of society (called opinion leaders, or influentials) who, in turn, either pass the message on by word of mouth to persons who consult them or utilize the message in the advice or information which they pass on to their circle of influencees.

Certain sociological studies, some of which are summarized below, contain information on mass communication as *social process*. First, we discuss the concept of opinion leaders and their linkage with the mass media.[5] We then examine two recent studies on the flow of news or information within a community—and again highlight the role of people in the mass communication process.

Informal Communication and the Mass Audiences

CASE #1: OPINION LEADERS IN AN ELECTION CAMPAIGN The earliest sociological recognition of the importance of individuals in mediating between the mass media and the general public was part of a pioneering study of voting behavior conducted by Paul Lazarsfeld and his colleagues during the presidential campaign of 1940.[6] Some of the background of this study helps to understand subsequent research on opinion leaders.

These researchers were primarily interested in discovering how and why people decide to vote as they do. In exploring this problem, Lazarsfeld and his colleagues introduced a new research method, the *panel technique,* by which the same people were repeatedly interviewed over an extended period of time. The panel technique represented an innovation in public opinion research for, among other things, it permitted the researcher to study the *development* and *change* in opinions and attitudes on-the-spot. He could detect persons who changed their minds, almost at the moment of change, and then study intensively the factors leading to the change (or to stability). In this instance the study consisted primarily (although not entirely) of interviews with a core panel of 600 persons in Erie County, Ohio, who were interviewed once each month from May to November, that is, just prior to and throughout the election campaign.

The researchers were also interested in determining the impact of the political campaign itself, including its mass media components, upon changes in voting intention. To their surprise (for one would have predicted the opposite), there was very little evidence of direct influence of the campaign in changing people's votes. This is not to say that the campaign had no effect whatsoever, or that on occasion it did not convert voters. But the basic impact of the mass campaign was to reinforce the original voting intention of some citizens and to activate latent predispositions of others.

A partial understanding of the tendency of the campaign to reinforce existing political preferences comes from data on the patterns of exposure to communication during the campaign. People were very *selective,* tending to pay attention to those materials which reflected their original predispositions. Republicans, for example, were more likely to expose themselves to Republican campaign messages and to media supporting their party than they were to heed the Democratic side of the campaign, and vice versa.

The reinforcement effect can be understood also in terms of the political homogeneity of social groups. The study showed repeatedly that people voted "in groups" in the sense that persons belonging to the same church, family, social clubs, and similar institutionalized groups tended to vote alike. The tendency toward political homogeneity of social groups can in turn, of course, be partially explained by the fact that people living under similar social and economic conditions are likely to share similar needs and interests and to interpret their experiences in similar political terms. But a fuller explanation must also take into account the importance politically within these groups of personal influence through face-to-face contacts. For example, "whenever the respondents were asked to report on their recent exposure to campaign communications of all kinds, political discussions were mentioned more frequently than exposure to radio or print." [7] It was in the discovery and analysis of such effective personal contacts that the concept of opinion leader, and a new hypothesis —the two-step flow hypothesis, developed.

In its most general form, the phrase *opinion leaders* refers to individuals who, through day-to-day personal contacts, influence others in matters of decision and opinion formation. Opinion leaders are not necessarily the formal leaders of the community or persons holding positions usually accorded social prestige. Each stratum of society seems rather to have its own group of opinion leaders. In the study under consideration, political opinion leaders were found in about equal proportions among professionals, clerks, skilled workers, and retired persons; and in varying proportions among all other occupational levels represented in the sample. How, then, is the researcher able to identify or recognize opinion leaders? This is a more complicated and difficult problem than it might seem at first glance, yet it had to be solved before information could be gathered on the connection between opinion leaders and mass communication.

It might seem that opinion leaders could be identified simply by asking people to whom they turn for advice or for help in making up their minds on various issues. In practice, however, this procedure has a major drawback—it assumes that all, or a representative group, of the opinion leaders so identified by respondents is available for study. In small communities or "closed societies" (such as a residence college) this procedure might be feasible. But for studies in which social research must be based upon small representative samples of larger populations, the method is no longer practicable. For it would turn up names of opinion leaders who could not be reached because they were not included within the sample; and conversely, many other opinion leaders might go undetected if the people whom they influenced were not also in the sample to identify them. What was required was some way to identify the opinion leaders among the people about whom most information had been and could be collected—those already in the sample. If properly drawn, a sample is a good cross section of the community from which reliable generalizations can be made.

A workable solution to this problem rests on the ability of opinion leaders within a sample to *identify themselves* for the researcher. This is not to say that they would name themselves "opinion leaders" or "influentials"; nor does it even imply self-consciousness or awareness of their leadership role. Rather, since the concept of opinion leadership refers to behavior, it means simply that these people are able to report whether or not they have been asked for advice or have given their advice to someone. From the respondents' own reports the researcher is able to specify the opinion leaders.

Thus, near the middle of the election campaign, each member of the panel was asked two questions: (1) "Have you tried to convince anyone of your political ideas recently?" and (2) "Has anyone asked your advice on a political question recently?" For the purposes of the study, anyone who answered "yes" to either or both of these questions was a self-designated opinion leader. Ancillary information and observations were obtained to support the validity of these identifications, but the key classification rested upon these two reports on behavior.[8]

Because the voting study was well under way before the full importance of opinion leaders was discovered, intensive analysis of their characteristics and role was not possible. However, this investigation provided some suggestive evidence about opinion leaders and set the stage for subsequent studies of personal influence. First, as noted above, opinion leadership was found to be distributed throughout the social structure, suggesting that personal influence flows not only from "top to bottom" within the society but also horizontally within social classes or other status groups. Second, the opinion leaders turned out to be especially alert, interested, and active politically. For example, six of every ten leaders said that they had a great deal of interest in the current election, in contrast with only one of every four non-opinion leaders. Third—and especially significant from our point of view—opinion leaders were more fully exposed to the mass media campaign than were non-opinion leaders. Opinion leaders were more likely than non-leaders to have read specific magazine articles about the campaign, newspaper stories and columns about the election, and to have listened to radio speeches, news reports, or political conventions. Furthermore, they were heavy users of the mass media regardless of their interest in the election—that is, opinion leaders were more likely to use the media than even those non-leaders who were equally interested in the election. Fourth—and most important—there was evidence that the opinion leaders used the ideas and information obtained from the mass media in the advice or information they passed on to their followers:

> In the present study we found that one of the functions of opinion leaders is to mediate between the mass media and other people in their groups. It is commonly assumed that individuals obtain their information directly from newspapers, radio, and other media. Our findings, however, did not bear this out. The majority of people acquired much of their information and many of their ideas through personal contacts with the opinion leaders in their groups. These latter individuals, in turn, exposed themselves relatively more than others to the mass media.[9]

This suggestion that information flows from the mass media to the opinion leaders and from them to the mass audience is expressed in the hypothesis of a *two-step flow of communication*. We shall return to it later.

CASE #2: PATTERNS OF INFLUENCE IN A SMALL TOWN
Further study of community influentials was conducted by Robert Merton, whose research focused on interpersonal influence and communications behavior in a small local

Eastern community of about 11,000 persons.[10] To locate
the influentials, Merton asked his informants to name
people to whom they turned for advice or help when
making personal decisions (selection of furniture, educational plans, choice of a job) and to name persons who
were generally asked for advice on these matters. Several
hundred names were obtained, several dozen of which
were found to have been mentioned four or more times
by the informants—these constituted the opinion leaders
or influentials for purposes of the study. Further information was gathered from the original respondents and from
direct interviews with more than half of the leaders, concerning their communications behavior, the situation in
which they exerted influence, and so on. As suggested by
the study design—that of gathering a wealth of information from a small number of key persons—this research
was exploratory, aimed at the discovery of important
hypotheses about interpersonal influence in a community.
The researchers hoped initially that their data would help
to identify the types of people regarded as influential by
their neighbors, to gain clues to the methods through which
they became influential, and to determine how their
patterns of communication behavior are related to their
role as influentials.

In the course of interviewing the townspeople and some
of the influentials, Merton and his colleagues made an
important discovery which has extended our knowledge
about opinion leaders in general and about the link between them and mass communications in particular. It
became evident that the entire concept of "the influential"
is inadequately specific, for there was no such single type
who stood apart from the general people in the community.
Rather, there seemed to be different types of influentials,
at least two of which were evident among the town's
opinion leaders. Merton identified these as *local* and
cosmopolitan influentials. The chief criterion for separating
the two types was their orientation toward their town,
the local influential being preoccupied essentially with

community affairs, the cosmopolitan influential being also concerned with the larger world, national and international, and its problems.

Once this distinction was made, a considerable part of the research centered on detecting similarities and differences between these two types of influentials. For example, the localite was more likely to be a native son of the community while the cosmopolitan had been more mobile and was a relative newcomer to the town. Local influentials were also more concerned with knowing a large number of townspeople, while cosmopolitans were more restrictive in their associations, tending to form friends with people on the same status level. And local influentials were more likely to participate in voluntary associations designed for making contacts and friends, while the cosmopolitan tended to belong to organizations which focused on special skills or interests, such as hobby groups and professional societies.

Local and cosmopolitan influentials also differed markedly in their communications behavior. Both types, to be sure, used the mass media more than did the average person in the community. Nevertheless, they differed in their communications tastes and in the uses to which they put the communications material. Consider, for example, their patterns of magazine reading. Both types of influential read magazines more than the average citizen. But the cosmopolitan leader was a heavier user, especially of news magazines. Merton explains this difference in terms of the functions magazines serve for each type of influential. For the cosmopolite, magazines in general, and news magazines in particular, are an important link with the outside world, providing information that helps to reduce his sense of cultural isolation and enables him to maintain his leadership on non-local topics. For the localite, on the other hand, news magazines are luxuries since they do not contain much material about local affairs—the topics upon which he may be called for an opinion. Similarly, although the localite read more newspapers, they were local ones, while the cosmopolite was more likely to be a regular reader of one of the metropolitan New York papers. Or, to move to a different medium, the localites' interest in radio news was limited primarily to straight newscasts, while the cosmopolites preferred news commentators and analysts who could help them to interpret events.

Of the many other illuminating points about influentials brought out in the study, one has particular relevance here. The discovery that there were at least two major types of influentials in the community raises the possibility that there might be more. Merton speculates about this possibility and advances the hypothesis that the local influential seems to be polymorphic. That is, his connections in town (upon which rests his influence) cover several different fields, and he can exert influence in a variety of spheres of life. On the other hand, Merton suggests, the cosmopolitan's influence is more likely to be monomorphic, that is, restricted to the field in which he is consulted as an expert—national or international politics, ladies fashions, world business, or some other subject. Support for Merton's hypothesis that opinion leadership in such matters tends to fall into several hands is found in the study to which we turn.

CASE #3: PERSONAL INFLUENCE IN A LARGER CITY   In the spring of 1945 a panel study of opinion leadership was conducted among a random sample of 800 women in Decatur, Illinois, a town of about 60,000 people. The results of this study were published in 1955 in a volume by Elihu Katz and Paul Lazarsfeld, entitled *Personal Influence*.[11]

Four problems occupied the researchers throughout this study. First, they were interested in determining the *impact* of personal influences as compared with the impact of the mass media in four areas of common decision-making: marketing, fashions, public issues, and (what was then still common) choice of motion pictures. Second, they investigated *characteristics* which differentiated opinion leaders from non-leaders in these four areas, especially in terms of the leader's position in the life cycle (for example, young woman or matron), socio-economic status, and patterns of gregariousness. Third, the researchers investigated the *flow* of influence—whether it went, say, from the older women to the younger, or from the rich to the poor. Finally, they studied the ways in which personal influence was tied to the mass media, that is, what the communications habits of opinion leaders were and how much they, in turn, were influenced by the mass media. Only the first and last areas of investigation concern us here.

First, let us consider the relative impact of personal *versus* mass communications. In order to study impact the researchers decided to analyze the role played by the several media in effecting recent changes in opinions or behavior among the members of their sample. For example, women were asked whether they had changed their hair styling or their way of dress recently; if so, they were asked a series of questions designed to detect the impact of mass and personal communications upon this decision.

How can one determine whether one medium or another has greater impact upon a person's decision? The concept of impact is a complicated one. For example, does the fact that one medium *reaches* a larger audience than another mean that it has greater impact? Not necessarily, for the communication that reaches the smaller audience may be more influential in affecting decisions than is the communication with the greater coverage, and vice versa. At least two factors are at work here—coverage and persuasiveness. Coverage can be measured in a variety of standardized ways. But impact cannot; so a new measure had to be invented. It consisted of a simple *index of effectiveness* which took into account both the amount of exposure achieved by the several media and the relative role each played in the decision itself.

The index is based on the answers to three types of questions. First, a general question was asked which permitted the researchers to identify the media having a *specific influence* on the decision. A woman might be asked, "How did you come to make this change to the new fashion?" She might then refer to conversations with other women or to something she saw or heard in the mass media. After obtaining an account of all the specific influences upon the decision, the interviewer would ask an *assessment* question, permitting the respondent to evaluate these influences on her decision, as, for example, "Summing up now, what was the most important thing in causing you to make this change in fashion?" To which the woman might answer, "The story I read in *Vogue*." Finally, a check list of various media to which the woman might have been *exposed* was presented to her to determine whether or not she was exposed to these influences, regardless of their degree of impact upon her decision. Sample questions included, "Did you hear someone talk about this fashion?" "Did you see someone wearing it?" "Did you see it in a magazine?" and so on.

The numerical value of the index of effectiveness is the proportion of persons who assess a particular medium as being most influential in their decision-making on some subject to the total number of people making that decision who report being *exposed* to that medium. In a simple equation:

$$\text{Index of Effectiveness} = \frac{\text{Effective Exposure}}{\text{Total Exposure}}$$

An example should clarify the procedure. Of all the women in the study who had recently shifted brands of food or household items, 117 (about 30 per cent) had heard some radio advertising about the product. About the same number (116) had seen some newspaper advertising about the product. Hence both media being compared here had equal *total exposure* among the brand shifters. But 29 of the shifters who had heard radio advertisements named this medium the most important influence on their decision; only 8 of the brand shifters who had seen newspaper advertising considered it the most important influence. The index of effectiveness for radio then, in this case, is 29/117, or .25; the index of effectiveness for newspapers is 8/116, or .07. The two media achieved equal coverage among the changers but radio advertising in this instance was more effective than newspapers, as evaluated by the changers.

These technical features of evaluating impact should give the reader sufficient information to interpret the meaning of the index, as well as provide the flavor of some of the operations involved in such research. With this background, a few of the findings may be summarized.

In three areas of decision-making under study (marketing, fashions, and motion picture selection) personal contacts had greater influence upon the decision-makers than any of the mass media studied, as measured by their index of effectiveness. For example, in marketing decisions, contacts with friends, relatives, or neighbors had an index of effectiveness of .39, in contrast with an index of .25 for radio advertising, .07 for newspaper advertising, and .07 for magazine advertising. Similarly, in choices of motion pictures the index of effectiveness for personal contacts was .33, for magazines .14, and for newspapers .06. These figures do not mean that the mass communications had no effect; on the contrary, sometimes the mass media played an important contributory role in the decision-making and occasionally they played the decisive role. But the data do underscore the relatively greater impact which face-to-face communications have upon decision-makers.

Why should personal communication be a more effective means of persuasion than mass communication? In their earlier study of voting behavior Lazarsfeld and his colleagues suggested five advantageous characteristics of personal relationships.[12] First, personal contacts are more casual, apparently less purposive, and more difficult to avoid than mass communications. Many people are highly selective of mass communications, avoiding materials that go against their personal opinions or in which they are not interested. But people are less likely to anticipate the content of the personal communication or to take steps to avoid it. Second, face-to-face communication permits greater flexibility in content. If the communicator meets resistance from his audience, he can change his line of argument to meet their reactions. Third, the direct personal relationships involved in face-to-face communication can enhance the rewards for accepting the message or argument and the "punishment" for not. Fourth, some people are more likely to put their trust in the judgment and viewpoint of persons whom they know and respect than in the impersonal mass communicator. Fifth, by personal contacts the communicator can sometimes achieve his purpose without actually persuading the audience to accept his point of view. In voting, for example, a forceful party worker or a friend may get individuals to go to the polls and vote without actually altering or activating their interest in the campaign or their position on the issues.

In the Decatur study, Katz and Lazarsfeld emphasize the advantage of the interpersonal aspects of face-to-face communication in affecting marketing, fashions, and movie selections. The mass media depend primarily on the *content* of their communications, especially on whether the content makes the object or viewpoint presented attractive to the audience. Personal communications, on the other hand, influence people not only through what is said but also by personal *control*, in which the source of the directive is as important as the content itself. "People can induce each other," write Katz and Lazarsfeld "to a variety of activities as a result of their interpersonal relations and thus their influence goes far beyond the content of their communication." [13]

Let us now consider a few of the findings about opinion leaders, their communications behavior, and data bearing on the hypothesis of a two-step flow of communications. Opinion leaders were identified in the Decatur study, as in *The People's Choice*, through their answers to questions about their role in giving advice. For example, each woman was asked both in June and in August, "Have you recently been asked for advice about what pictures to see?"

If she said yes, detailed data were gathered about the incidents. Also each woman was asked in August whether she thought she was more or less likely than other women in her circle of friends to be asked her advice on such topics. From the answers to these questions an index was constructed which separated opinion leaders from non-leaders in each area of opinion under study.

Examination of the characteristics of these opinion leaders gave strong support to many of the hypotheses suggested by the earlier studies on personal influence by Lazarsfeld, Merton and others. For example, just as, in *The People's Choice,* opinion leaders on politics were found in all walks of life, so were Decatur's opinion leaders on marketing, fashion, public issues, and motion pictures widely distributed. Each stratum of society seemed to have its own group of opinion leaders. Furthermore, each sphere of life usually had different people serving as opinion leaders, just as there were separate influentials for local and cosmopolitan issues in Merton's study. There was no evidence of a generalized leadership factor which might make an opinion leader in one area of life more likely to be a leader in others. Considering three areas (fashions, marketing, and public affairs), the researchers found that only 3 per cent of the women in the study were opinion leaders in all three fields at the same time; 10 per cent were leaders in two fields; 27 per cent were opinion leaders in just a single area. Hence, at least in areas which do not restrict themselves to local issues, personal influence appears to be monomorphic, as had been suggested in Merton's research on cosmopolitan leaders.

What were the communications habits of opinion leaders? Here, too, several of the relationships noted in earlier studies received corroboration. The opinion leader's generally high exposure to mass media was again documented. Leaders in every sphere of influence tended to be more highly exposed to mass communications than were the non-leaders. They read more books and magazines than non-leaders, for example, and attended the movies more often. Second, the selective nature of exposure to the mass media was again evident—leaders read magazines which dealt with their speciality, fashion leaders being more likely to read fashion magazines than either non-leaders or opinion leaders in other fields. And mass media that reflect a cosmopolitan orientation (as out-of-town newspapers and national news magazines) were more often read by opinion leaders in the fields of fashion and public affairs, than by leaders in marketing or motion pictures—giving support to Merton's observation that such media are selected because they serve a specific function for the opinion leader. Third, some support for the two-step flow of communications was obtained:

> So far we have seen that the opinion leaders tend to be both more generally exposed to the mass media, and more specifically exposed to the content most closely associated with their leadership. Presumably this increased exposure then becomes a component—witting or unwitting—of the influence which such influentials transmit to others. As a result of these findings, the idea of the "two-step flow of communication" gains credence.[14]

Of course, the term "two-step" is more heuristic than definitive. That is, it suggests that some—by no means all —communication content reaches a mass audience indirectly through the mediating efforts of opinion leaders. But it is quite possible (as, indeed, some of the findings in Decatur and in subsequent studies would indicate) that there may be more than two steps in this process. Sometimes opinion leaders on some topic look in turn, to other people for information and advice on that subject. And some of these second-level influentials may depend on the mass media while others turn to still a third circle of opinion leaders for advice; and so on. That the communications process may be more complex than originally suggested by the term "two-step flow" does not detract from the important reconceptualization signified by that term.[15]

Some recent research on opinion leaders has also explored the role of interpersonal influence in the flow of information among such select segments of the society as physicians, but such research has only secondary relevance for our study of *mass* communications.[16] Two other studies have applied a different strategy to the study of mass communication as a social process. The first traces the spread of a news item throughout two neighborhoods; the second traces the flow of information from mass-distributed leaflets within several communities.

CASE #4: HOW NEWS GETS AROUND Important contributions to our knowledge about the role of mass communication in modern society come from research on how people learn of important or routine news events. This type of research gives evidence on such questions as which media provide initial and supplementary information, how long it takes for the news to flow to various segments of the population, and what part personal contacts play in the communications process. An example of modest and well executed research along these lines is a study made in Seattle by two sociologists, Otto Larsen and Richard Hill, of the diffusion of news about the death of Senator Robert A. Taft.[17]

Senator Taft died in New York City on a Friday morning in July, 1953, at 7:30 by Pacific Coast time. Seattle received its first news of the Senator's death by wire service at 7:45. Within fifteen minutes Seattle's six major radio stations had broadcast the news; the story was on television at 10:45 (the first telecast of the day); and available in the newspapers downtown at 2:30 P.M. (several hours later than would be normal for Seattle because of a newspaper strike). On Saturday the researchers interviewed approximately one hundred and fifty men and women living in a housing project for faculty members of the University of Washington. On Monday evening they also obtained nearly one hundred and fifty interviews with residents of an interracial working-class housing project near the industrial section of Seattle. These two sets of interviews provided the basic data for the study.

The news was diffused widely and quickly. By the time of the interviews fully 88 per cent of the faculty community and 93 per cent of the laboring community knew of Senator Taft's death. Among the knowers, 50 per cent in the faculty neighborhood had gotten the news by 10:46 —only three hours after the wire service reports reached Seattle. In the workers' neighborhood the median time of learning about the event was somewhat later—4 P.M. In both communities men heard the news a little later than the women. On the average, people who heard about the event from the radio learned it earliest; next were those who got the news by word of mouth, followed, in turn, by television viewers and the newspaper audience.

Within both the faculty and working-class communities the highest proportion of persons reported first hearing about the death on the radio. But beyond this similarity the patterns of obtaining the news differed greatly between the two communities. Among the faculty group the second highest proportion cited interpersonal communication as their first source of the news, while relatively few first learned of the event from television or the newspaper. And this pattern held for both men and women. Among the workers, on the other hand, television was the second most important source of news of the event, while news-papers and interpersonal communications nearly tied for third and fourth places. Here, however, the communica-tions habits of men and women differed. By and large, the working-class women first heard of Senator Taft's death by radio and television, 8 out of every 10 women so reporting, as compared with only 5 out of every 10 working men. Working men were more likely to have gotten the news from newspapers and word-of-mouth com-munication. Once they had heard the news, about 6 out of every 10 faculty members and 3 out of 10 workers searched around for more information about the event. The faculty group used radio as the immediate source of supplementary information, while the laboring group turned to the newspaper.

What light does the study shed on the connection between personal and mass communications? The study has several broad implications. First, it emphasizes the importance of primary groups in personal communication about events—those who first heard the news by word of mouth usually got it from another family member, in the faculty community, or, in the case of the men in both communities, from a co-worker. Second, there is strong evidence that people do more than just listen to mass-communicated news—they talk about it with friends, relatives, neighbors, and co-workers. At least 80 per cent of the people who learned about the Senator's death discussed it with others, each person talking to about three others, on the average. Not all of these conversations resulted in spreading the news to those who had not already heard it; in fact, only about 15 per cent, of the reported conversations did so. Nevertheless, of those who first heard about the event from one of the mass media, from 12 to 29 per cent passed this news on to another person, in addition to holding non-informative conversations about the topic with others. Hence the study provides additional support for the two-step flow hypothesis.

CASE #5: PROJECT REVERE—THE FLOW OF LEAFLET IN-FORMATION   When we talk about the mass media we do not ordinarily think of leaflets. But under special conditions, such as war, this form of communication increases in prominence. Though usually leaflets fall on the periphery of our attention—along with roadside billboards, skywriting, sound trucks, and other marginal media—they can, under certain conditions of construction and distribution, fit our criteria for mass communication nicely. Their messages are distributed rapidly and publicly to a large, heterogeneous, and anonymous audience. And usually leaflets are the expendable products of a large organization rather than the work of an isolated artist or writer.

In 1951 the United States Air Force commissioned the Washington Public Opinion Laboratory at the University of Washington to study scientifically some of the conditions under which leaflets are most effective. The research included field experiments involving the systematic dropping of leaflets by airplane over selected communities, followed by intensive interviewing of residents of these communities. The study (called Project Revere, probably because the theme of one of the major leaflets used was "Be a modern Paul Revere") extended over a period of three years. The significant phase of the research for us has been recently reported by two sociologists, Melvin De Fleur and Otto Larsen, in *The Flow of Information*.[18]

The major experiment that De Fleur and Larsen report involved dropping leaflets, at varying ratios of leaflets per person, over eight communities in the vicinity of Seattle. The towns were relatively small, with populations that ranged from about one thousand to eighteen hundred each. The leaflets stated that one raid by an enemy bomber could disrupt regular channels of communication and that leaflets could provide an alternative channel; therefore, each person who found them should "Be a modern Paul Revere" by filling out and mailing an attached questionnaire postcard and passing on extra leaflets to others. We need not go into further details of the design except to note that the results of the drops were determined from two types of questionnaires: (1) the detachable leaflet questionnaire which was supposed to be mailed to the Project office by anyone who found a leaflet, and (2) a standardized questionnaire used in interviewing a random sample of the population in each community about three days after leaflets were dropped.

De Fleur and Larsen's work focused on two major tasks: (1) the development of a mathematical model which relates stimulus intensity (ratio of leaflets to population) to diffusion of the message, and (2) an analysis of

the mechanics of message diffusion throughout the communities. We shall summarize some of the major points
from this latter analysis here.

First, the authors explored the relationship between the
diffusion of the leaflets and such elementary social characteristics of the population as age, sex, and family size.
As a measure of diffusion, they separated the community
members into two types: people who gave evidence during
the interviews that they knew about the leaflets (for example, by being able to name part of the content of the
message) and those who did not. In general, it turned
out that a higher percentage of children (16 years old or
younger) in the communities knew about the leaflets than
of adults. Furthermore, the greater exposure of children
was most pronounced in communities which had received
a low ratio of leaflets per person. Also, it was discovered
that adults who lived in "large" households (having more
than two members) were more likely to have learned
about the leaflets than adults from smaller households,
and again this was more pronounced in communities receiving a low ratio of leaflets. Finally, there did not appear
to be any significant difference in the proportion of men
or women, or boys or girls, who knew the message. To
summarize, the leaflet message was more likely to reach
children than adults, and to reach adults from large households than small; and each tendency was more pronounced
when there was a relative shortage of leaflets in the community.

How did people learn about the leaflet message? Three
ways were possible: (1) by picking up a leaflet from the
ground; (2) by receiving a leaflet from someone else; and
(3) by hearing about the leaflet from someone else. (To
help the experiment, the other mass media agreed not to
mention the leaflets until after the experiment was con-
cluded.) Again, the researchers compared people of different ages, sex, and family status with respect to how the
message spread—whether through the process of physical
diffusion (picking a leaflet from the ground), or through
social diffusion of the tactual or oral type. They were

also able to ascertain the stimulus conditions under which these relationships might vary.

Social diffusion was found to be much more important in communities which received a low ratio of leaflets. But even in communities of high stimulus intensity, social diffusion accounted for nearly half of the contacts with the leaflet message. And social diffusion was important to both adults and children. It was especially important to adults from larger households in communities which received relatively few leaflets. The importance of social diffusion is underscored by the authors:

> The most important finding with respect to the means by which the message knowers first came in contact with the leaflet content is that under both [i.e. high and low] stimulus conditions the leaflet operator was greatly dependent upon *social diffusion*, or interaction in the community, for the spread of the leaflet message. Under low stimulus conditions nearly two-thirds of the message knowing was achieved through social channels, while under high stimulus conditions nearly one-half of the knowers learned through social contact in the community.

> Thus, we know that a considerable degree of the diffusion accomplished must be accounted for by what amounts to at least a *two-step flow of information*.[19]

The authors' findings on the nature of social diffusion as it affects different types of community members (as, for example, persons from large households) are too numerous to be reviewed here. However, one discovery deserves special mention because of its immediate importance to our knowledge about opinion leaders and persons who can mediate between the mass media and the general public.

Throughout the study the active role of *children* in the process of social diffusion was noted time and again. Children, for example, were especially important as agents for passing on the leaflets, both to one another and to adults—not only to adults who were family members or neighbors, but also to mere acquaintances. On the other hand, children were less likely to be active in the oral diffusion of the message. Passing the message on by word of mouth usually involved adults as transmitters to both adults and children. Thus we have another case in which different types of people function as mediators between the mass communication and the public, as was noted in research that was previously cited on voting, small towns, marketing, fashions, public affairs, and movie going.

Together with these other studies, this experiment with leaflets adds support to the broad hypothesis with which Project Revere began: "The effectiveness of the mass communicative act depends in determinable ways on the degree to which the media are linked to the interpersonal networks and on characteristics of those networks." [20]

Other Aspects of the Mass Audience

During the past several decades considerable research has been conducted in the field of audience analysis, including studies of the social characteristics of audiences for certain media, overlap among the media's audiences, the nature of fans and abstainers, and the communications habits of people of similar or different social backgrounds. Of the many topics covered by audience research three are of special sociological interest: overlap among the audiences for mass communications; social characteristics of the audiences; and selective exposure.

First, a variety of studies have demonstrated a tendency toward "all-or-none" exposure to mass communications.[21] This phrase does not mean that people either use all of the media or none. Rather, it means that people who are heavy users of one medium are also likely to use others fairly regularly; and people who avoid one medium are also likely to restrict their use of others. Nor does the "all-or-none" pattern imply that there is no competition for audiences. Indeed, the invasion of television into the leisure-time market has sharply cut into the time audiences formerly spent on radio, movies, and other activities. Nevertheless, certain people tend to be more media-minded than others and manage their leisure hours so as to permit some regular use of all of the mass media available to them.

Second, there is evidence that the audiences for the various mass media differ significantly in their social characteristics (perhaps more than they differ in any recognizable personality traits).[22] For example, college educated adults are more likely to be regular readers of books and magazines than are others. On the other hand, movie audiences (and especially fans) are likely to include an extraordinarily high proportion of young people; frequent movie attendance is less likely to be a correlate of formal education.

In addition to these special characteristics of each mass audience, at least one interesting pattern can be discerned. Programs that can be classified as more serious than light (classical music, discussion of public affairs, forums—as distinguished from popular music, comedies, mysteries) appeal to older persons and people with more formal education. Serious communications appeal least to younger people and people with less formal education. The relation between "serious" communication tastes and such primary social characteristics as age and educational background cannot be explained simply in terms of the greater reading skills of the highly educated, for the preferences also carry over to such "spectator" media as radio and television, in which the audience need only listen or watch.

Program preferences reflect, in part, a more general trait of audiences, called *selective exposure*. People select the mass media and content which they believe will be most interesting and will reinforce their initial views, opinions, and experiences. And to a great extent the interests and predispositions which guide audiences in their self-selectivity have roots in the group structure within which each audience member lives. Lazarsfeld has described this phenomenon as follows:

In all the fields that have been touched by communications research the self-selection of audiences plays a considerable role. People with political convictions read the newspapers that correspond to their opinions. People with hobbies read the sections of the newspaper which report on these hobbies most fully. This seemingly trivial observation becomes more interesting as we add to it certain corollary findings which can be gleaned from a variety of studies. It has been found, for instance, that people are inclined to read the same news items in newspapers which they have already heard discussed on the radio. In general, they do not look for information on new topics in magazines but for more information on topics with which they are already acquainted.

. . . In general, then, people look not for new experiences in the mass media but for a repetition and an elaboration of their old experiences into which they can more easily project themselves. If we assume then that the types of experiences they have had are determined more by their social roles and context rather than by their psychological traits, it is not surprising that we find primary characteristics [age, sex, educational classification] so dominant in the correlations which communications research has unearthed.[23]

Thus our analysis of the mass audience returns once more to the persistent role of social variables in accounting for audience behavior. We will do well to keep in mind the importance of these social factors when we examine some effects of mass communication on the individual and his society, in Chapter 5. Our immediate concern, however, is with the *content* of mass communications—a topic sufficiently important to warrant a chapter for itself.

4

Cultural Content
of American
Mass Communications

Why Study Mass Media Content?

Every American schoolboy is familiar with the programs, stories, features, and other materials that constitute our mass media. Why, then, should such widely recognized elements of everyday life as comic strips, soap operas, and television shows require scientific research? Isn't our common first-hand knowledge about these subjects sufficient for sociological analysis? Why should we *study* mass media content?

At least three reasons for the systematic study of content can be offered. First, despite the frequency of our exposure to mass communications, our experience is both limited and selective. For example, it is impossible for any of us to witness all of the television programs broadcast even in our own communities during an average day or week. Furthermore, because we are highly selective in our exposure, our knowledge about what is being transmitted is biased by our personal tastes. Hence only a systematic monitoring of all broadcasts would give us a representative view of the range of television output. Second, we tend to over-generalize from our particular communication experiences. For example, if we happen to witness several television programs which feature violence, we are inclined to assume that most television fare reflects violence. Finally, in our daily exposure to mass communications we are seldom motivated to analyze the sociologically meaningful aspects of the content. For example, in viewing television for our personal entertainment we are not ordinarily prompted to note or analyze the social class or occupational characteristics of the heroes, heroines, villains or villainesses on the screen. Content analysis can provide us with the necessary perspective and the accurate and sociologically important data on the products of American mass communication.

What is content analysis? One expert defines it as "a research technique for the objective, systematic, and quantitative description of the manifest content of communications." [1] Perhaps the key terms in this definition are "objective" and "systematic." Objectivity requires that the categories of analysis be so clearly and operationally defined that other researchers can follow them with a fairly high degree of reliability. For example, analysis of the social class membership of characters in a comic strip or radio serial requires a clear specification of the criteria by which the social class membership can be identified and classified. "Systematic" requires that *all* of the relevant content be considered in terms of the meaningful categories. Thus systematic analysis is distinguished from critical or analytical reading, viewing, or listening, in which the reviewer may select any part of the content that supports his argument. For example, if you believe that television programs portray scientists in an unfavorable light, you probably can look at a few television shows and find stories in which the scientists appear villainous, dishonest, or generally despicable. At the same time, someone with an opposite opinion can just as easily find equally dramatic examples of scientists who are portrayed heroically. Neither of you would be conducting a content analysis, however, for each has *selected* cases to illustrate his point. Obviously what you need is an unbiased overview of the relative frequency of favorable and unfavorable characterizations of scientists—an overview that can come only from classifying *all* the scientists in a representative sample of television programming.

The uses of content analysis are many and varied. Bernard Berelson, in a recent authoritative text on the technique, summarizes studies using content analysis not only to supply direct data on the characteristics of the content, but also to permit inferences about the nature of the communicator, the audience, and effects.[2] Research on content characteristics includes studies of trends, international comparisons, propaganda techniques, style, and so on. Sometimes content is analyzed to provide insights into its producers—their intentions, or political or psychological states. Occasionally content is taken as a clue to the nature of audiences—their values, likes, and dislikes. Finally, content is at times interpreted in terms of its presumed effect upon the audience or society.

It is important to remember, however, that content analysis itself provides no *direct* evidence on the nature of the communicator, audience, or effects. Therefore great caution must be exercised whenever this technique is used for any purpose other than the straightforward description and analysis of the manifest content of the communication. If, for example, we find that scientists are portrayed unfavorably on television, we cannot use this as evidence that television writers or producers *intend* to portray scientists unfavorably. Nor can we claim that these unfavorable stereotypes will deflect students from scientific careers. Such interpretations of the content in terms of probable motives or effects go beyond the available data. Ideally, to know what motivated the portraits we would need research on the communicators themselves; to discover the consequences of the stereotypes we would need direct audience research. In the absence of direct evidence on communicator or effects, however, researchers sometimes prefer to make inferences about them from content analysis rather than speculate on such matters with no data at all.

For a complete and detailed survey of subjects that

have been investigated through content analysis the reader should consult Berelson's *Content Analysis*. In the remainder of this chapter we will discuss findings from a few illustrative content analyses applied to two sociologically interesting topics: (1) the types of characters who serve as cultural heroes or villains in our mass media, and (2) the types of television programs broadcast during an ordinary week in metropolitan America.

Society's Heroes and Villains

High on any list of content analyses that provide clues to our cultural heroes is a study of biographies in popular magazines, conducted by Leo Lowenthal nearly twenty years ago.[3] We noted earlier that one sign of high status in a mass society is to be singled out for attention by the mass media. Perhaps an even greater sign is to be selected as the subject for a biography in one of the popular media. To some extent, biographies are the life histories of cultural heroes or villains, from whose experiences the reader can learn lessons of success or failure. Whether or not the reader actually accepts the characters as role models is, of course, a separate empirical question, unanswerable by content analysis. But knowledge about the kinds of persons selected for biographical attention should be valuable as an aid to understanding American culture as reflected by the mass media.

Lowenthal analyzed a systematic sample of all biographies appearing in two popular magazines—*Collier's* and the *Saturday Evening Post*—for the first four decades of the twentieth century. Sample years were taken for the period 1900 to 1940; then an intensive analysis was made for the year 1940-1941. By that time biographies had firmly established themselves as popular literary types, rising from an average of 36 per year in the two magazines at the beginning of the century to 125 during 1940.

Undeniable trends emerged during the forty-year span. Above all, it was clear that the idols selected for biographies near the end of the span were very different from those at the beginning. Men of "production," in the spheres of politics, business, and the professions, dominated the earlier period; men of "consumption," primarily from the field of entertainment, achieved prominence in the modern time. Even among the biographies of entertainers Lowenthal noted a shift of attention away from those who might be placed in the classical or "serious" arts (literature, fine arts, dance, classical music, theater) toward heroes of the popular arts. To illustrate, fully 77 per cent of the entertainers written about in the biographies prior to World War I were persons from the "serious" arts. During the 1920's the proportion dropped to 38 per cent. By 1940-1941 less than one in ten biographies of entertainers dealt with the "serious" type.

There was a shift in the qualitative content of these biographies too. Older popular biographies contained a good deal of information on the subject's character development, early history, and behavior that had led to success. Modern biographies tend to gloss over the details of character development and give more attention to private life and leisure-time activities. Often the stories of success in current biographies are told in terms of the hero's inherent character traits plus a series of hardships and "lucky breaks" along the road to success. Lowenthal argues that such a formula is hardly useful as a model for others. It defines success as largely an accidental and irrational event, and reflects a degree of normlessness about patterns for getting up in the world.

Many other qualitative (and quantitative) differences between earlier and modern biographies are documented in the study. One warrants special mention here because it suggests an important function of modern biographies for the average reader. Lowenthal discovered a tendency for the new biographies to stress the consumer habits, likes and dislikes, of the popular heroes. In interpreting this new focus (an interpretation which, of course, must go beyond the data of the content analysis itself), Lowenthal suggests that it provides the reader with a frame of reference about success within which he is less likely to suffer by comparison with the "great" persons of our times:

> . . . the distance between what an average individual may do and the forces and powers that determine his life and death has become so unbridgeable that identification with normalcy, even with Philistine boredom, becomes a readily grasped empire of refuge and escape. It is some comfort for the little man who has become expelled from the Horatio Alger dream, who despairs of penetrating the thicket of grand strategy in politics and business, to see his heroes as a lot of guys who like or dislike highballs, cigarettes, tomato juice, golf and social gatherings—just like himself. He knows how to converse in the sphere of consumption and here he can make no mistakes. By narrowing his focus of attention he can experience the gratification of being confirmed in his own pleasures and discomforts by the great. The large confusing issues in the political and economic realm and the antagonisms and controversies in the social realm—all these are submerged in the experience of being at one with the lofty and great in the sphere of consumption.[4]

Many of the trends noted by Lowenthal in the biographies up to 1940 appear to be even more pronounced today. For example, an unpublished study of biographies in the *Saturday Evening Post* from July 1956 to June 1957 found an even greater proportion of idols coming from the world of entertainment, and almost all of these from such popular media as radio, television, and motion pictures.[5] As in Lowenthal's cases, few clues were given about character development and patterns of success. And the emphasis on private lives and habits continued.

Heroes and villains are conceptualized somewhat differently in another study, drawn from a content analysis of all the television programs broadcast in New York City during the week of January 4, 1953.[6] In part of the study, conducted by Dallas Smythe for the National Association of Educational Broadcasters, 86 drama programs originally produced for television and telecast during that week were analyzed, first in terms of the settings and the kinds of characters in this television "world," then in terms of the social and psychological characteristics of the heroes, villains, supporting characters, and of the qualities attributed to occupational groups in the stories.

Although occasionally they took place in foreign places or in other historical times, the dramas given during the period studied mainly portrayed contemporary but fictitious settings within the United States. Men outnumber women in the casts by a ratio of about 2 to 1. Very young people (under 20) and very old (over 60) are underrepresented in the stories, which focus primarily on persons at the height of the courting and child-bearing ages, who are employed or employable. Such higher white-collar positions as managers and professionals are heavily overrepresented at the expense of the routine white collar and blue collar jobs. Service workers and household workers also are overrepresented. Most of the TV characters are law-abiding, healthy and sane individuals. They are most likely to be white Americans (4 times out of 5), occasionally Europeans (English, Italian, or French), and rarely Negro (only 2 per cent of all characters shown during the week). Absent altogether, during the week, were individuals representing India, Africa, and Asia, with the exception of a few Chinese.

Within this somewhat distorted portrait of the world, how do the heroes and villains appear? Male dominance continues: heroes outnumber heroines 2 to 1, and villains outnumber villainesses by almost 4 to 1. Heroes are usually younger than villains; the average villainess is older than the average villain; the average heroine is younger than the hero. Smythe suggests that in these portrayals villains represent the menace of the older generation who have more social power than the heroes, but are physically and sexually on the wane.

White Americans have the edge over foreigners, providing proportionately more (83 per cent) of the heroes and fewer (69 per cent) of the villains. The foreigners who are heroic, however, are more likely to be women than men, while among Americans heroes outnumber heroines 3 to 1. Only ten Negroes appeared during the week, two as heroic characters and eight in supporting roles, neither heroic nor villainous. In general the supporting roles in the dramas are distributed among American whites, foreigners, and minority races in proportion to the incidence of these groups in the total TV population.

As might be expected, heroes are usually law-abiding and villains lawbreakers. But to say merely that this is expected is to underrate the sociological significance of presenting heroes as supporters of the normative structure of the society. The innovator who by-passes society's laws to achieve his goals is unusual among our heroes. Robin Hood and Mike Hammer are the exceptions in a world in which most heroic characters operate within the law. In TV life, disregard for the norms is usually not heroic but undesirable.

After describing the social characteristics of the heroes and villains, the researchers applied a special technique (called *semantic differentiation*) to explore the personalities of the central characters and the degree of stereotyping in the casting.[7] Specially trained monitors rated each leading character on sixteen scales based on pairs of antonyms. One scale, for example, contained the antonyms "fair" and "unfair." The monitor scored each central character according to whether he appeared to have the quality of being more fair or unfair. Ten of the scales used were valuative in nature, requiring the judge to rate the character on such qualities as bravery, or cowardice, attractiveness, or ugliness. Two were measures of inner power—strength and hardness. Four referred to such personality traits as sharpness, quickness, and smartness, which might be relevant for activity.

Heroes were typically evaluated as having personalities that conformed closely to the ideals of our culture—very brave, attractive, honest, clean, kind, fair, loyal, admirable, and moderately happy and generous. Villains had typical personality patterns that were almost the direct opposite of the heroes—very ugly, deceitful, cruel, unfair, despicable, and moderately sad, dirty, miserly, and disloyal. Villains were rated slightly more brave than cowardly, but not as brave as heroes. Villains had at least as much inner power as the heroes, however, being rated almost as high as the heroes in strength and higher in hardness. Heroes tended to be slightly sharper, quicker, and smarter than the villains. With a few exceptions these general patterns of heroic and villainous personalities applied to both male and female characters.

Using the same scales, the researchers next examined the personality profiles of such occupational groups as business executives, public officers, criminals, white-collar workers, teachers, lawyers, journalists, doctors, scientists, entertainers, farmers, domestic servants, and housewives. With rare exceptions all of the legitimate occupational groups (that is, excluding criminals and illegal business executives) were shown to be more in line with community ideals than not. However there were wide differences in the characteristics associated with these groups. For example, among the professionals the journalists were most favorably characterized, being especially honest, strong, hard, and quick. On the other hand, scientists were rated as the least brave, kind or fair of the professionals and almost the slowest, dullest, and softest. Teachers, though clean, kind, and fair, were nevertheless the slowest, dullest, weakest, and softest professionals. Lawyers were rated "dirtiest." Doctors and entertainers had favorable personalities. Among the other groups, only the criminals and illegal business executives had predominantly unfavorable personality characteristics. Interestingly, housewives' personality profiles were basically similar to those of the American-white heroines in the stories.

Stereotyping of characters was measured in terms of degree to which the apparent personality of the members of each group conformed to the typical pattern for that group. By this criterion journalists were the most stereotyped, doctors were least. Other groups subject to stereo-

typed portrayals were lawyers, teachers, and law-enforce-
ment officers.

Whether the audience is aware of the subtle differences
in the personalities associated with the occupational groups
in the dramas or the degree of stereotypic presentation
cannot be answered by content analysis. Nor can the impact of the portraits be assessed without other kinds of
studies. Nevertheless, scientific and systematic analyses of
content such as Lowenthal's qualitative analysis of biographies and Smythe's quantitative analysis of television characters go far in enlarging our knowledge about the heroes
of our popular culture. They provide us with a factual
background against which possible effects can be more
realistically considered.

A WEEK OF TV IN METROPOLITAN AMERICA   At least three
out of every four homes in America have television sets.
It is estimated that the typical viewer spends three to five
hours of his leisure time daily watching the television
screen.[8] What kinds of programs are available to him in
an average week?

There are several ways to find out what is being broadcast in metropolitan America. Published program guides
or television station logs should provide some useful clues
to the general programming. But often it is difficult to
know the exact nature of a program from its title. Furthermore, many elements of television content might not be
apparent from published guides (for example, the number
and type of advertisements). There is no substitute for
direct viewing of the telecast as a method for learning
about its content.

In order to provide the public, the broadcasting industry,
and the Federal Communications Commission with an
accurate survey of television programming, the National
Association of Educational Broadcasters sponsored a series
of television monitoring studies in several big cities from
1951 through 1954.[9] All the television broadcasts in a
sample week were watched and classified by a trained
staff of monitors according to the nature of the program,

the time it lasted, the length and frequency of advertisements, and other pertinent data. (We have already noted the analysis of characters performed in one of these monitoring studies in New York.) The content of New York City television programs for a week in January was analyzed in 1951, 1952, 1953, and 1954. Other studies were conducted in Los Angeles (May 1951), New Haven (May 1952), and Chicago (August 1951). Some of the findings from the New York studies provide data on trends in television programming in addition to an accurate overview of an ordinary week.[10]

All television programs were classified into one or another of three broad types: entertainment, information, and orientation. Entertainment included such programs as general drama, westerns, comedy drama, variety, quiz contests and crime drama. Information programs were those devoted to such topics as arts, crafts, cooking, science, shopping, and travel. The orientation category covered public events, public issues, religion, personal relations, and public institutional programs.

From 1951 through 1954 most television time in New York was devoted to entertainment, in 1954, for instance, about 78 per cent being so spent. Certain time segments throughout the day were more dominated by entertainment than others. The domestic hours (sign-on to 5 P.M.) had about 72 per cent of their time programmed for entertainment; the children's hours (5 P.M. to 7 P.M.) had 81 per cent so used; the adult hours (7 P.M. to 11 P.M.) 83 per cent; and the late hours (11 P.M. to sign-off) 72 per cent. And entertainment, from 1951 through 1954, usually meant drama.

About 17 per cent of total program time was devoted to information programs and 5 per cent to orientation shows. Again there were variations throughout the day, information programs being more prominent during the daytime domestic hours and the late evening, orientation shows during the children's hours.

Heavy emphasis on entertainment is not unique to American television. A similar pattern has been observed in Great Britain, although the BBC devotes more of its total program time to information and orientation programs than American stations. When, in August 1953, a week of BBC television was monitored and programs classified, 66 per cent of the time was found to be spent on entertainment; 24 per cent on information; and 10 per cent on orientation. Subsequent analyses of the program guides for BBC and for the newly formed commercial Independent Television Authority—while not strictly comparable to the direct monitoring—also demonstrate the frequent use of television for entertainment. In one week in January 1956, for instance, the distribution of BBC time was about 67 per cent for entertainment, 24 per cent for information, and 9 per cent for orientation. During the same week about 78 per cent of the ITA program time went into entertainment, 14 per cent to information and 8 per cent to orientation.[11]

In terms of the four major communications activities listed in Chapter 1—surveillance, interpretation, cultural transmission, and entertainment—television in the Anglo-American countries would appear mainly devoted to the last named activity at the expense of the others. News programs, for instance, which might be taken as the most direct index of surveillance, occupied only 6 per cent of total broadcast time in New York in 1954. Explicit cultural transmission, in the form of general information and instruction in such activities as cooking, arts, crafts, shopping, or personal care took up about 9 per cent of program time. Editorial activity or correlation, as expressed in such programs as discussions of public issues, accounted for less than 2 per cent of program time.

Although the time devoted to public issues was brief, researchers decided to do a small exploratory analysis of these shows of such great potential importance to public opinion. Their findings, though only preliminary, are nevertheless suggestive and interesting.[12] Each discussion of a public issue was rated according to the degree of rationality of the arguments used, the diversity of views presented, and the impartiality of the discussion. Half of the discussions contained mostly rational appeals; about 13 per cent had essentially emotional arguments; the rest were mixed. More than one view was presented in 45 per cent of the discussions, and in at least 30 per cent of the discussions many views were presented. In not quite one-half of the discussions the audience was left to judge the issue for itself; in about one-fourth of the cases there was an effort to "sell" views to the audience; the remainder were fairly impartial but contained some "selling."

Next a comparison was made between the public issues discussed on any television show (whether classified as a public issue program or not) and the topics found on the front pages of New York's seven largest daily newspapers during the week of the study. The findings are difficult to interpret. There was some overlap in topics covered, to be sure. Five out of the twelve specific topics listed constituted about the same percentage of issues in both media. At the same time there were some differences. Newspapers gave much less attention to the economy and the recession, for example, than television. The Berlin conference and the refusal of repatriation by captured American soldiers, major topics for the newspapers, drew much less attention in television discussions. Of course how much overlap is desirable in topics discussed by the newspapers and television remains an open question. Some persons might feel that different foci of attention for each of the mass media helps assure an airing of all current topics and thus proves functional for democracy. Others might feel that overlapping coverage provides greater opportunity for expressing many different views on the major issues of the time. Perhaps some combination of common and diversified selection of public issues serves both purposes.[13]

Two other aspects of the television content analysis warrant brief mention here. They touch on issues that are often at the center of public concern and criticism: advertising and violence on television.[14]

Just how much time is spent on advertising? The answer requires a distinction between two kinds of television advertising: primary and secondary. Primary advertising consists of commercials that interrupt the program itself; secondary advertising accompanies but does not interrupt the program, such as product plugs worked into the show in the form of jokes, displays, and trademarks. From 1952 through 1954, during the weeks studied in New York, 18 per cent of all program time was spent on advertising. This means that, on an average, a little over ten minutes of every broadcast hour was devoted to advertising. Not quite three quarters of the advertising in 1954 was primary; the rest was secondary advertising worked into the program itself. The amount of time spent on advertising varied with the time of day and the product or service sponsored. When the sponsor's product was jewelry, approximately 27 per cent of total program time went directly into primary advertisements and 42 per cent of program time contained secondary advertisements; sponsors selling dairy products, on the other hand, spent about 12 per cent of their program time on primary advertisements and 1 per cent on secondary.

That there is violence on television is so obvious to the casual observer as to be hardly worthy of note. Less available to casual observation, however, is information on how much violence there is, during what time of day, on what kinds of programs, and within what contexts. Data in answer to these and similar questions were gathered for the first time in 1952 and extended during the 1953 and 1954 analyses in New York. Violence, for purposes of the study, meant physical or psychological injury, hurt, or death addressed to living things. The analysis counted both acts and threats of violence; the agent of violence; the method used; and the context within which the violence occurred, classified as either (1) a tension-producing or thrilling situation; (2) "normal," routine violence or violence not accompanied by tension-producing stimuli; or (3) sham violence or humorous violence. Context was significant since presumably acts of violence are interpreted according to the situation in which they occur: violence in slapstick comedy has a meaning different from violence in a crime drama.

Someone was injured or threatened by violence once in every six minutes of program time during the week of analysis in New York in 1954. In total there were over 7,000 acts or threats of violence observed. Almost all of the violence occurred in the entertainment type of program, especially on children's shows, which had an average of 38 acts or threats of violence per hour. In most cases (eight out of every ten) human agents were responsible for the violence, rather than animals or other non-human sources.

In what kinds of situations did violence occur? About one-fifth was found in a tension-producing or thrilling context—presumably these are the situations most likely to have an impact upon the audience, although questions about effects are still problematic. Not quite half of the violence occurred in a neutral setting; the remaining violence (not quite one-third of the total) was in a humorous or sham context. In children's programs, relatively little of the violence occurred in a tension-producing context and a good deal of it (59 per cent) occurred in humorous situations.

The impact of televised violence upon the adult or child audience remains unknown. Again here, as in other problems involving the evaluation of effects, much more research directly on audience members themselves is needed. It is the general question of the social effects of mass communications to which we turn.

5

Social Effects
of Mass Communications

Anyone who wants to invite a quarrel about mass communications need only assert an opinion about their social effects. Charges, denials, and countercharges color almost every public discussion about media impact in the editorial columns of our daily newspapers, in testimonies before Senate Committees, in critical essays in the "little magazines," and elsewhere. Typical controversial questions are: Does the show of violence and crime on television cause juvenile delinquency? Do certain comic books encourage sadism? Can adult information campaigns raise the level of public knowledge about national and international issues? Can the mass media be used to persuade the public to safeguard its health through check-ups for venereal disease, heart ailments, and other disorders? Can a newspaper crusade swing an election? Does international propaganda help to prevent war? Widely different opinions can be found on each of these and similar questions involving the effects of mass media on public taste, morals, politics, adult education, crime, and other social matters. And perhaps only within the restrictive framework of scientific discussions are such topics handled with dispassion.

Why is there so much controversy about these matters? Two salient causes are the shortage of conclusive scientific evidence on media effects and the tone of social urgency that often surrounds the questions about effects. A brief discussion of these two conditions serves as a useful background for more detailed treatment, in the rest of the chapter, of the effects of mass communications on juvenile delinquency, mass persuasion, and the democratic process.

Scientific research on communications effects is far too scarce to provide the information needed for an understanding of the subject. As one scholar testified recently concerning the effects of television on children, "The effect of television on children is controversial not because some people are against crime and others for it; it is controversial because so little is known that anyone can inject his prejudices or his views into the debate without being proven wrong." [1] Even the available research findings are not always unequivocal, especially if one tries to interpret them as evidence for or against particular courses of social action.

Often there is an apparent social urgency in discussions about the effects of mass media, especially concerning such salient and insistent social problems as juvenile delinquency, crime, and public morality. This social anxiety makes people impatient with a slow, objective, and dispassionate scientific orientation toward the problems and encourages a search for immediate opinions and social remedies.

Sometimes the mass media themselves are perceived as social problems by laymen and social critics, a turn of events that is worthy of some speculation. Lazarsfeld and Merton have identified four sources of the public's concern about mass media.[2] First, many people are alarmed by the mass media's ubiquity and potential power to manipulate Man for good or evil. The average person feels he has little or no control over this power. Second, some people fear that economic interest groups may use the mass media to insure public conformity to the social and economic *status quo*, minimizing social criticism and weakening the audience's capacity for critical thinking. Third, critics argue that the mass media, in accommodating large audiences, may cause a deterioration of aesthetic tastes and popular cultural standards. Finally, some people criticize the mass media as having nullified social gains for which reformers have worked for decades. For instance, through the cumulative effort of many men, and women, people at last have shorter working hours, greater opportunities for free education, and social security. Presumably these are the conditions necessary for enjoying the fine arts, acquiring more education, studying our cultural heritage. But what do people do with their newly acquired leisure time? They view comedy and variety shows on television, listen to rock-and-roll or hillbilly music on the radio, go to crime and horror movies, and so on. Hence leisure time and its uses pose new "social problems" to be solved.

The absence of definitive research and the presence of public (sometimes national) concern over the issues involved make the need for additional sociological research especially pressing. At this time any discussion of social consequences must be provisional. Our treatment of the topics in the following sections is admittedly selective. Several comprehensive reviews of the literature on effects are listed in the bibliography, however, for the reader who wants to explore any topic more thoroughly.

Mass Communication, Delinquency, and Socialization

Whether or not any of the mass media actually contribute to delinquency is a subject on which both public and expert opinion is currently divided. Gallup Polls have shown that about seven out of every ten American adults think that juvenile delinquency can be blamed at least partially on such media as crime comic books and mystery programs on television and radio.[3] But three out of ten people do not share this opinion; and even if they did, consensus on the matter need not mean that public opinion is correct. Experts likewise disagree. Recent testimonies submitted to Senator Kefauver's special Senate subcommittee to investigate juvenile delinquency in America illustrate the divergent judgments of psychiatrists, child psychologists, clinicians, and others.[4]

Much of the disagreement among professionals centers on whether there is any *significant* connection between media exposure and delinquent behavior and, if so, whether the connection is causal, contributory, or deterrent.

Some experts are convinced that certain mass media have harmful effects that are so obvious as to be self-evident. Fredric Wertham, a noted psychiatrist, makes the following comment on certain comic books:

> They contain such details as one girl squirting fiery "radium dust" on the protruding breasts of another girl ("I think I've discovered your Achilles heel, chum."); white men banging natives around; a close up view of the branded breast of a girl; a girl about to be blinded. Whenever I see a book like this in the hands of a little seven-year-old boy, his eyes glued to the printed page, I feel like a fool to have to prove that this kind of thing is not good mental nourishment for children! [5]

Other professionals, who have reservations about mass media contribution to delinquency, are worried lest too much public alarm about mass media divert attention from such other causes of delinquency as disturbed family relationships, the influence of neighborhood gangs, individual emotional disturbances, and insecurity.

One current view is that communication content which to the observer seems harmful actually might be functioning as a deterrent of delinquency—permitting youth to work off their aggressions vicariously, for example, as they watch scenes of violence in the movies. Another viewpoint, shared by several professionals, is that such materials may affect different people differently. The average adolescent may be unharmed by scenes of violence, for example, but an emotionally disturbed child or gang may be stimulated by them or have delinquent tendencies reinforced. Highly relevant research on frustration, aggression, and communications behavior is being conducted at Harvard University by Eleanor Maccoby and her colleagues. In 1951-1952 lengthy interviews were conducted with several hundred mothers in the Boston area, to determine whether children who are highly frustrated in life spend more time watching television than those who are not.[6] During the interviews information was obtained about parental behavior that might restrict or frustrate the child —strict methods of training, severity of punishment, permissiveness in areas of sex and aggression. Each mother also estimated the daily length of time her children spent watching television. It was then possible for the researchers to examine the average number of hours of daily television viewing for children who were subject to varying degrees of frustration in the home. If the use of TV reflects a need for vicarious satisfaction through fantasy, then those children who are most frustrated should use it most. Such a relationship was obtained for middle-class children; but in the lower-class homes it was not.

Finally, some people consider the risk of certain communications harming juveniles great enough to warrant social action, even though there is inadequate evidence on the subject. This viewpoint is exemplified in a portion of the conclusions and recommendations from the report on television and juvenile delinquency by the Senate Subcommittee on Juvenile Delinquency:

> Members of the subcommittee share the concern of a large segment of the thinking public for the implications of the impact of this medium of visual presentation upon the ethical and cultural standards of the youth of America. It has been unable to gather proof of a direct causal relationship between the viewing of acts of crime and violence and the actual performance of criminal deeds. It has not, however, found irrefutable evidence that young people may not be negatively influenced in their present-day behavior by the saturated exposure they now receive to pictures and drama based on an underlying theme of lawlessness and crime which depict human violence.
>
> When considered in the light of the evidence that there is a calculated risk incurred through the repeated exposure of young boys and girls, even of tender age, to ruthless, unethical forms of behavior, the subcom-

mittee believes it would be wise to minimize this risk
insofar as possible . . .[7]

Since the views on the effect of mass media on delinquency are so divergent and the present evidence so
inconclusive, it seems best to avoid a premature judgment
on this complicated issue and to turn instead to the broader
question of *how* the media might influence the total character of youth.

Public attention often centers on two methods by which
the mass media seem to affect youth. First, certain content
might *over-stimulate* the audience, as through scenes about
sex, passion, and violence. When such content violates
public norms it often becomes the object of reform movements, sometimes within the communications industry itself. One of the earliest publicized reforms of the comic
book industry under its first "czar," for example, was a
regulation against exaggerated portrayals of women's
breasts and other physical characteristics on comic book
covers. (The daily press referred to this as giving the
comic books "that Dior look.") A second charge is that
certain mass communications encourage deviant behavior
by children who *imitate* the actions of the characters.
Usually this claim is documented by references to stories
such as that of a youngster who hanged himself amid
comic books portraying such behavior or a child injured or
killed while trying to fly like superman.[8] Admittedly such
cases are the exception rather than the rule—not every
child who reads about hanging attempts it on himself or
other children. But they dramatize a media influence that
needs further analysis and research: the possibility that
some (and perhaps all) children *learn* something about
life, and how to cope with it, from the mass media. More
formally, they direct our attention to the role mass media
play in the *socialization* of modern children and adults.

Socialization is the process by which the individual ac-
quires the culture of his group and internalizes its social
norms, thus making behavior begin to take into account
the expectations of others. It is important to emphasize

that socialization is an ongoing process—extending from childhood through old age. Some norms as, for example, basic rules about food and eating, are transmitted to the individual as a child; others, such as norms about courting, are postponed until later. Some matters involve continuous instruction throughout life. Responsibility for socialization is ordinarily located in specific people or institutions, depending on the normative area involved. Early toilet training is usually directed by the mother, while later occupational training is supervised by other members of the occupation or specialists in a vocational or professional school, or on the job. Socialization is usually deliberate, but occasionally it occurs inadvertently when the individual picks up cues about social norms without special instruction about them.[9]

Some part in the complex process of socialization is taken by the mass media. Either deliberately or inadvertently, the individual at various times in life probably obtains some of his social norms from them. It is important to remember, however, that mass communication is only one of many sources of socialization for the child and the adult. Just what specific part the mass media play is still unknown.

What kinds of data do we need to map out the role of mass media in socialization? We need, obviously, data on the communications behavior of people of various age levels. Much evidence is already available on this subject —we know, for example, that even very young children spend a great deal of time with the mass media, either alone or in the company of their family or friends. But more detailed information is desirable; longitudinal studies of changes in media habits with age would be especially useful. Second, more evidence is needed on the use of the media (advertently or inadvertently) as sources of social norms. Several studies suggest that people consciously refer to the media as normative sources. For instance, some women believe that they can get prescriptions for living and solving personal problems from daytime radio serials; there is also evidence that older people begin to use the media less for sheer entertainment and more for their serious informational functions.[10] Third, we need more information on the extent to which people absorb social norms from the mass media—consciously and unconsciously, directly and indirectly (from others who have acquired norms from the media). Here data are needed, for example, on audience identification with characters who serve as role models or reference figures for values and behavior. We need to know more about the relative rank of the mass media as normative sources among such other major agents of socialization as the family, school, and peer group.

The two studies summarized here illustrate research touching upon some of the problems of socialization mentioned above. One is a study of children's identification with the characters in radio space serials; the other is a study of the impact of a radio program intended to help socialize adolescents.[11]

In the first study, by Robert Zajonc, a radio program about the adventures of a space rocket was played in different versions for two groups of children between 9 and 13 years of age. The program had two leading characters, Rocky and Buddy. Rocky was a power oriented character; he tried to solve problems through his authority and direct control over others. Buddy was an affiliation-oriented leader; he tried to handle problems by establishing affective associations with other people, being liked by them, being friendly or nice. One group of children heard a version of the program (Space Masters) in which the bulk of the perils the rocket ship faced were solved by Rocky and his power-oriented approach to interpersonal relations. The other group heard stories (Space Mission) in which Buddy, with his affiliative orientation, was more successful.

After the show the children were asked whether they would rather be like Buddy or like Rocky. Presumably the answers would indicate whether the listeners identified with a character on the basis of the kind of person he seemed to be (tough vs. friendly) or on the basis of how successful he was, regardless of his methods. With only a few exceptions the listeners chose the character who was successful. That is, listeners to Space Masters wanted to be like Rocky; those who heard Space Mission wanted to be like Buddy. Furthermore, in response to a question about why they would rather be like one character than the other, most children answered in terms of the personal attributes of the successful figure. Those who heard the version in which Buddy was successful found his affiliative attributes most attractive; listeners to the version which portrayed Rocky's success found power attributes desirable (although with some exceptions). Finally, the researchers considered whether the children had made the values represented by the heroes part of their own code, asking the children which goal would be more important for them if they were the captain of a space ship: making sure that everybody gets along together, or making sure that everybody obeys orders. Children exposed to the affiliative-oriented programs chose the first goal, while those who heard the power-oriented version were more likely to choose the second.

This study should be regarded as exploratory rather than as definitive. The cases involved are small and the population limited. And, as the authors indicate, the effects measured may have been short-lived ones rather than basic changes in the value systems of the children.

Another study, by Raymond Forer, of the impact of a radio program called *Mind Your Manners,* is of special interest to the topic of socialization for two reasons. First, the program chosen made a deliberate effort to socialize its adolescent audience. Advice was given by a panel of "typical" teen-agers who discussed personal problems submitted by the listeners. Second, the study investigated whether the audience followed the norms prescribed by the panel and what would happen if these norms conflicted with those prescribed by family, friends, or other agents of socialization.

Forer distributed questionnaires to a sample consisting of 2700 Connecticut students of high school age. Those students who had a knowledge of the program (a majority of the sample) were asked a series of additional questions designed to measure its impact. Most of these students thought that the advice given on the program was usually very good; 7 out of 10 said they would ordinarily follow the advice.

What would happen if the program's advice differed from that given by others? Listeners were asked if they would follow the advice given by the program instead of that given by their father, for example, or by their mother. The alternatives covered ten primary group relations and three mass media. Of all the primary groups, by far the most powerful agent of socialization in competition with the radio program was the nuclear family. About 9 out of every 10 adolescents would take the advice of their mother or sibling(s) instead of that of the program, and nearly as many would follow their father's advice. Religious leaders were ranked fairly high, with over 8 out of 10 students giving their advice priority. The advice of an older friend, grandparent(s), aunt or uncle would be taken first in 2 out of 3 cases. Advice from such institutional figures as teachers and recreation leaders would be followed instead of the program's in only 4 out of 10 cases. But a fairly large proportion of respondents (nearly 50 per cent) would adhere to the program's advice in preference to that of their teen-age friends—an anomalous finding in view of current notions that the face-to-face adolescent peer group is one of the most important influences on youth. Finally, the program's advice would be preferred to that offered by such other mass media as books, teen-age magazines, and newspaper columns. This study reminds us, then, that the impact of the mass media must be evaluated in relation to the total complex of social relationships within which the audience member functions before, during, and after his exposure to the medium.

Before closing this discussion of media and socialization, it is essential to emphasize again the need for data on the functions and dysfunctions of *mass* communication as an instrument of socialization. We need to know, for instance, what difference it makes if social norms are acquired through the impersonal mass distributed communications rather than through such primary sources as the family, friendship, or work group. We need data on the extent to which socialization by mass communications standardizes culture throughout all social levels and geographical regions of the society. The role of mass communications in the creation and perpetuation of a youth subculture should be explored. And we need to know the extent to which mass socialization changes the quality of the normative content transmitted, as well as whether it strengthens or weakens social control in the mass society. Research on these and similar questions will enhance our sociological perspective and understanding of the role of mass communications in the overall process of character formation as well as in such a specific area as juvenile delinquency.

Successful Campaigns and Mass Persuasion in a Democracy

During the first half of the twentieth century many citizens of the Western world, and especially those in democratic nations, have become increasingly concerned about the political and social power of mass communication. This concern, in its most general form, expresses itself in such broadly phrased questions as: Do the mass media really have any effect on public opinion? On elections? On attitudes toward such basic democratic values as freedom and equality? Underneath these questions may be a fear that the individual and the public can be manipulated by those who have access to the mass media. Stated slightly differently, the issue becomes: Are our opinions, attitudes, knowledge, and behavior so vulnerable that they can be changed by what we see on television, read in the newspapers, hear on the radio, and so on?

Thus phrased, the question is easily answered, but the answer is seductively simple. Of course the media affect the public. We know this from common observation and from a wealth of systematic research evidence. After all, one's perception of the world around serves to guide many of his opinions and much of his behavior. And in modern societies a large part of the picture of the world comes through mass communications. But the danger of this simple answer is that it may forestall our recognition of the equally important fact that not *all* mass communications are successful in affecting opinions, attitudes, knowledge, or behavior. The process of mass influence is far from automatic, and the public's role in this process far from passive. Consider as examples the following two public spirited campaigns.

CASE #1: A WAR BOND MARATHON   During World War II, Kate Smith, broadcasting over the CBS radio network in an 18 hour marathon, during which she repeated appeals every few minutes, obtained pledges from the audience for approximately $39,000,000 worth of U.S. Government bonds. In a similar marathon a year later she sold $112,000,000 worth of bonds in 18½ hours.[12] Both events were remarkable demonstrations of the potential power for mass persuasion available to one individual using only one major avenue for mass communication.[13]

CASE #2: A PUBLIC INFORMATION CAMPAIGN   In 1947 several public organizations, including the American Association for the United Nations, began an intensive six-month mass communications campaign in Cincinnati, Ohio, presenting information about the U.N. and world affairs. The Cincinnati Plan was to provide a social demonstration of how a large community could become informed on world issues through a mass educational campaign. Many communications facilities of Cincinnati were used extensively throughout the six months—features were run in newspapers and over the radio, special pamphlets, signs and posters were distributed, meetings and speeches were arranged.

What was the net result of the campaign? Apparently little of social consequence was achieved. At the request of the campaign's sponsors an evaluation of its impact was made by the National Opinion Research Center of the University of Chicago. Using data gathered from a random sample of Cincinnatians before and after the campaign, the researchers detected no significant influence on the public's knowledge, interest, opinions, or behavior concerning the U.N. or world affairs. For instance, before the campaign fully 30 per cent of the adults in Cincinnati could not say what the main purpose of the U.N. was or even indicate familiarity with its general concern with keeping the peace. After the campaign 28 per cent of the Cincinnatians, judged by the same criteria, still were unacquainted with the U.N.—an educational gain of only 2 per cent of the public.[14]

With respect to serious communications campaigns, the Smith program illustrates success; the Cincinnati Plan illustrates failure. But both cases point to the conclusion that the critical consideration here is not *whether* mass media campaigns have any effect on the public, but under what *conditions* they do so. What are some of the factors —especially social and psychological—that help determine their success or failure?

For purposes of analysis it is convenient to view the communication process in several stages, starting with the formulation and transmission of a message through some mass medium, proceeding through a stage of audience exposure and immediate response or reaction to the message, and culminating in some short- or long-term effects. A breakdown in effectiveness at any stage during the process may cause the ultimate failure of a mass communications campaign. Our discussion will focus on the social and psychological factors affecting audience exposure, reactions, and effects.[15]

Audience coverage is an obvious precondition for effective communication. A variety of other factors also determine the effect of the message, but it cannot be influential at all if it does not reach a sufficiently large portion of its target. For instance, adequate physical output must be maintained in a form accessible to the public.

But there are other than physical requirements which must be met if a communication is to be effective. For clues to such requirements let us consider the Cincinnati campaign again. What went wrong?

In analyzing the dynamics of the Cincinnati campaign the researchers from NORC asked: How many people were exposed to the campaign during the six months? What kinds of people were reached? Who was missed? What effect did the campaign have on those people it reached? Just where in the total process of mass education did the campaign fail? Through the answers to such questions the major cause of failure could be pinpointed by the researchers. They found that the campaign had reached only individuals who were already predisposed to pay attention to it because of their initial interest in world affairs and the U.N. or because of their favorable attitude toward the U.N. Bear in mind that there was no dearth of communication output during the campaign, nor was the material inaccessible to the public. The campaign failed because it did not reach those most in need of its message from the point of view of the sponsors. That is, it did not reach the ill-informed, apathetic, or hostile people in the city.[16]

Was the behavior of Cincinnatians in this instance idio-syncratic—related perhaps to the content of this particular case of political education? No. As noted in Chapter 3, similar behavior has been observed in other studies of serious educational and propaganda campaigns in a variety of areas, for example public health programs and presidential election campaigns. Cincinnatians, then, were simply following the practice of *selective exposure*—a common and major obstacle to successful communication campaigns.

But unfavorable physical conditions and selective exposure are not the only barriers to communication. Two experts in public opinion research, Herbert Hyman and Paul Sheatsley, have recently codified some of the major reasons why information campaigns fail.[17] Hyman and Sheatsley identify five psychological characteristics of humans that affect their exposure to campaigns and their absorption of the message. First, repeated social surveys have revealed the existence of a hard core of chronic "know nothings"—people who know nothing about most topics with which a campaign might deal, and whose social and psychological make-up makes them especially hard to reach, no matter what the level or nature of information contained in the campaign. Second, there are large groups in the population who admit that they have little or no interest in the public issues around which campaigns are usually organized, an effective barrier since interest is a strong determinant both of exposure to and absorption of information. Third, people tend to expose themselves to material that is congenial with their prior attitudes and to avoid exposure to that which is not congenial. Fourth, there is selective perception and interpretation of content following exposure. People perceive, absorb, and remember content differently, according to such mediating factors as their wishes, motives, and prior attitudes. Finally, changes in views or behavior following exposure to a message may be differentially affected by the individual's initial predispositions and attitudes.

Dramatic evidence of selective perception and interpretation is provided in a study by Patricia Kendall and Katherine Wolfe for Columbia University's Bureau of Applied Social Research,[18] concerning reactions to a series of anti-prejudice cartoons. The cartoons satirized a highly prejudiced character, Mr. Biggott, who was depicted expressing hostility toward American minority groups in a variety of situations. The pictures were shown to 160 men. Detailed interviews, lasting from one to three hours, were held with each man to determine his understanding and reaction to the cartoons.

The interviews revealed that the anti-prejudice message was *misunderstood* by approximately two-thirds of the sample. Furthermore, many of the men not only misunderstood the message but actually reversed its meaning, and believed that the cartoons were designed to create racial disturbances and to intensify existing prejudices. The explanation of these misunderstandings is complicated. However, one finding is especially relevant for the discussion of selective perception. It turns out that the major correlate of understanding or misunderstanding was not a man's formal background (as measured by the amount of formal schooling he'd had, for example) but rather the presence or absence of certain predispositions to understand. Among the most important of these were the man's original prejudices and his awareness of the problem of prejudice in the world. To illustrate, among men who were themselves prejudiced and not concerned with prejudice as a social problem, three out of four were likely to misunderstand the cartoons.

Through laboratory and field experiments and through practical experience in propaganda and education, quite a bit has been learned about other factors that affect immediate response to communications.[19] Interpretation of these findings requires considerable caution, however. We never can be certain that the findings obtained under controlled conditions of an experiment or wartime field conditions would also appear under other circumstances.

Excellent social psychological experiments have been made in this area, among them the studies conducted by Carl Hovland and his colleagues at Yale.[20] Their research has shown, for example, that the audience's reactions to a message are affected by its image of the communicator —his social responsibility and intentions, his trustworthiness, and his orientation to education or propaganda. In general, people tend to resist messages coming from sources they regard with suspicion. A brief and partial description of one experiment by Hovland and Walter Weiss will illustrate this social psychological approach.[21]

The experiment was designed to test the influence of source credibility on communications effectiveness. Short articles were written about controversial topics—whether an atomic powered submarine could be developed, whether antihistamine drugs should be sold only by prescription, what Hollywood's future might be in an age of television— printed as if they were actual newspaper or magazine features, and given to two groups of college students. Half of the students received articles labeled with names of authors or magazines they would consider credible (*New England Journal of Biology and Medicine,* for example); the other half received articles whose supposed sources they would consider untrustworthy (*Pravda,* for example). The content of the articles was the same for each group, only the names of the author or source being changed.

From the responses to questionnaires given to the students before and after reading the articles, the researchers could measure reactions to the stories, the amount of information learned by each reader, and any changes in opinions about the topics. The crux of the problem was, of course, whether credibility of source had any effect on these three factors. Answers came from comparing the responses of the two experimental groups.

First, differences in the believed authorship resulted in marked variation in the students' evaluation of the arguments. That is, the same articles that were judged as fair by the group who believed them to be by a trustworthy author were evaluated as biased or unfair by the group who thought an untrustworthy person was the author. Second, there was no evidence that the image of the author affected the learning of facts; students acquired about the same amount of information from the articles regardless of whether they believed the author was credible or not. Third, authorship of the articles affected significantly their ability to change the audience's opinions on each topic. People were much more likely to change their views as advocated by the articles when they believed the author to be trustworthy than when they did not.

So much for immediate impact of the articles; but what of the longer-range effects? Hovland and Weiss measured the opinions of the students again one month after the experimental session. Especially interesting are their findings about the group which had originally been exposed to the communications from an apparently untrustworthy source. A sizable percentage of those students who had not changed their opinions immediately after reading the articles had subsequently done so, in the direction advocated by the message. This phenomenon of delayed conversion (which was also observed in experiments with Army training films during World War II) has been labeled the "sleeper effect." One explanation of it is that the message was initially unsuccessful because of suspicion toward the communicator rather than because of any deficiencies in the arguments used. During the month following the experiment there was a dissociation of content and source in the audience's minds. The information and arguments that they had heard, now no longer tainted by memory of the original untrustworthy source, were able to change their opinions. Subsequent experiments lend support to this hypothesis.

The Yale research group has also experimented with how effectiveness of communications is influenced by variations in the nature of the content and the audience situation. Experiments have been made with fear-rousing appeals, one-sided arguments, and with audience participation. The results underscore the importance of research on the long-term consequences of mass communications as well as on their immediate effects.

With so many social and psychological barriers to success, one may wonder how effective mass persuasion is ever achieved. Yet, under favorable conditions, the mass media can give a communicator great power. An illustration is the War Bond drive mentioned earlier in the chapter.

An excellent analysis of the social and psychological factors in the success of Kate Smith's marathon is presented in *Mass Persuasion* by Robert Merton, Marjorie Fiske, and Alberta Curtis.[22] Merton and his colleagues combined a content analysis of the themes in the broadcast with focused interviews with a sample of the program's listeners, some of whom had pledged to buy bonds. These detailed interviews were supplemented with a survey, of approximately 1,000 New Yorkers, which tested some of the hypotheses and observations from the smaller sample.

The researchers found Miss Smith's broadcast effective,

among other reasons, because of a combination of characteristics of the event itself, the public image of Kate Smith,
the themes employed, and the predispositions of the audience.

First, the campaign itself was defined, both by Kate
Smith and by the listeners, as a unique event. Against a
background of commercial radio programs and other common forms of advertising, the marathon stood out as
something extraordinary. It caught the attention of the
radio audience. Furthermore, by its very nature a marathon gave the communicator a variety of advantages, such
as by increasing the audience's motivation to continue
listening in order to hear the outcome and by permitting
arguments to cumulate and to be repeated in several forms.

Not only was the broadcast perceived as different from
ordinary commercial events but Kate Smith herself was
regarded as especially suitable for the role of bond sales-
man. The New York survey indicated that technical com-
petence in financial matters was not the main quality
people believed the role called for but such personal
qualities as sincerity, patriotism, and benevolence. Kate
Smith was, to many, a person especially endowed as a
moral leader, rather than simply as an entertainer or
business woman. Furthermore, the very act of conducting
the marathon validated her sincerity, as Merton puts it,
by the propaganda of the deed.

The themes in the broadcast were especially suitable to
the patriotic, sincere character symbolized by Kate Smith.
At no time during the marathon was there any emphasis
on the "profane" aspects of bonds—their value as financial
investments or their role in curbing inflation. Rather, the
program stressed the more sacred themes. Especially
prominent was the motif of sacrifice—by servicemen, by
other civilians, and by Kate Smith herself. Other themes
concerned participation in a common enterprise, competition between communities, familial values, the ease
with which a pledge could be made (simply pick up the
telephone), and Kate Smith's personal desire to make the
campaign a success.

Content analysis could identify the variety of themes used, but focused interviews with the audience were necessary in order to evaluate the themes' effectiveness. Not every theme had equal impact upon all members of the audience. Predispositions toward war bonds in general and the Third War Loan drive in particular seemed to make the audience members differentially responsive to one or another of the themes. For example, some listeners' orientation toward war bonds was fairly sentimental and emotional. Others were less involved. Some people had already planned to buy a bond during the Third War Loan drive; others had not. Those who had both emotional involvement and intent to buy may be considered the favorably predisposed members of the audience. They had only to be persuaded to buy the bond at that moment and from Kate Smith. For this group the facilitation theme (just pick up the telephone) seemed to have great impact, presumably because it saved them the effort of going out to buy their bond. Other themes appealed to persons with different predispositions.

Especially interesting is the process by which the group called the "susceptibles" were persuaded. These people had an emotional involvement in war bonds but had no intention of buying one from the drive. Their reluctance reflected in part their feeling that they were already doing their share through systematic purchases of bonds, perhaps through a payroll savings plan. (At the time there appears to have developed an informal social norm that a patriotic citizen was doing his share if he invested about 10 per cent of his income in bonds.) In convincing these people that their past behavior was insufficient, the themes of sacrifice apparently were most successful. By stressing the greater sacrifices being made by servicemen and other civilians, Kate Smith was able to overcome the audience's complacency, lower their self-esteem, and arouse some guilt feelings. The susceptibles came to the conclusion that they were not doing as much as other good citizens to help win the war. Miss Smith's own right to point up this deficiency and to call for greater effort from her audience was established by her favorable public image combined with the sacrifice she herself was making by conducting the marathon. Since it was clear that her actions exceeded the ordinary, she was not asking her audience to do more than she. Next she prescribed the new behavior that could raise the self-esteem of the audience and reduce guilt feelings—buy a *sacrifice* bond. Even the mechanism by which the deed could be performed was provided—simply use the telephone. Finally, as moral leader, she rewarded the new behavior by reporting on the progress of the campaign, citing dramatic incidents from the telephone calls received, etc.

Other factors contributing to the success of the broadcast, such as the fact that there was no counterpropaganda, are detailed in *Mass Persuasion*.

To the many social psychological factors that have been illustrated here through the work of Hyman, Hovland, Merton, and others we must remember to add such sociological variables as have been discussed earlier. For example, the social groups to which each audience member belongs or refers will influence his chances of being exposed to any media campaign, his perception and interpretation of the content, and its impact upon him. The social context sets limits also to the range of behavior any message can produce. For example, enemy troops stationed far behind the front lines can hardly surrender, no matter how persuasive the appeals of psychological warfare might be.[23] As another example, studies of Allied psychological warfare against the German Wehrmacht have shown that the early politically focused propaganda had little effect in terms of surrender of troops. Two social scientists, Edward Shils and Morris Janowitz, discovered that the German soldiers were held together less by any political dogma than by a tightly knit arrangement of primary groups within the Army.[24] Hence propaganda that stressed political themes had little impact. Few of the men could be persuaded to surrender because each was integrated into a primary group whose members depended upon one another for friendship and the other human satisfactions that sustain morale. There was little social possibility for desertion, except for those few soldiers who (for one reason or another) were social isolates, who had not been accepted and integrated into the primary group. Allied propaganda became more effective later when it abandoned the political emphasis and stressed such themes as individual survival, group survival, and the strategically hopeless position of some of the troops. Themes of individual survival appeared most successful among men who had become physically (hence socially) isolated from their units. Propaganda that utilized primary group pressures—for example, leaflets that persuaded the men to begin talking to one another about their military position, their desire to stay alive for their families' sake, and the possibility of honorable surrender—were sometimes quite effective.

These cases reemphasize the importance of viewing mass communications as functioning within the larger sociological perspective of the culture, social organization, and human groups. This has been a recurrent theme in the present chapter and, indeed, in the entire Study.

Some other aspects of the social effects of mass communications have been touched upon at other parts of the Study: the impact of mass communications upon voting, for example, was discussed in some detail in Chapter 3, with reference to face-to-face communication and opinion leadership. Of course, a complete treatment of social effects would consider many other topics, such as the meaning of mass communication for the democratic practice of trial by jury. To what extent does coverage of crimes by mass communication affect the probability of finding jurors who have not already formed a secret opinion about a case? Or how might radio and television coverage of a trial affect the behavior of witnesses, jury, lawyers, and other participants? Would such on-the-spot coverage jeopardize the trial system by turning each trial into a spectacle? Or would it enhance the proceedings by making the actions of the participants open to immediate surveillance by the public?

Here, as throughout the Study, our purpose has been

to suggest rather than to exhaust the sociologically ex-
citing aspects of mass communication. The reader who is
encouraged by this analysis to explore some topics further
will find the selected bibliography a useful guide to his
subject.

NOTES

CHAPTER ONE

1. For a summary of several cases of isolated humans, see R. M. MacIver and C. H. Page, *Society, An Introductory Analysis* (New York: Rinehart and Company, Inc., 1949), pp. 44-45.

2. C. A. Siepmann, *Television and Education in the United States* (Paris: Unesco, 1952), pp. 56-61.

3. *Variety,* November 12, 1952, as cited in *Television, A World Survey* (Paris: Unesco, 1953), p. 68.

4. H. D. Lasswell, "The Structure and Function of Communication in Society," in L. Bryson (ed.), *The Communication of Ideas* (New York: Harper and Brothers, 1948).

5. For an introduction to such sociological orientations as functional analysis, as well as to basic concepts, see E. Chinoy, *Sociological Perspective* (Studies in Sociology, New York: Random House, Inc., 1954), especially Ch. 5.

6. R. K. Merton, *Social Theory and Social Structure,* Revised edition (Glencoe, Ill.: The Free Press, 1957), Chapter I, "Manifest and Latent Functions."

7. An example of such an unanticipated consequence can be found in R. O. Carlson, *The Influence of the Community and the Primary Group on the Reactions of Southern Negroes to Syphilis* (unpublished Ph.D. dissertation, Department of Sociology, Columbia University, 1952).

8. B. Berelson, "What 'Missing the Newspaper' Means," in P. Lazarsfeld and F. Stanton (eds.), *Communications Research 1948-1949* (New York: Harper and Brothers, 1949), pp. 111-129.

9. R. K. Merton introduces the distinction between

local and cosmopolitan influentials in "Patterns of Influence: A Study of Interpersonal Influence and of Communication Behavior in a Local Community," in Lazarsfeld and Stanton, *op. cit.*, pp. 180-219. Parts of this research are summarized in Chapter III of the present Study.

10. P. Lazarsfeld and R. Merton, "Mass Communication, Popular Taste and Organized Social Action," in Bryson, *op. cit.*, pp. 95-118. Several of the ideas about the functions and dysfunctions of mass communication which are outlined in the present chapter are derived from this insightful and instructive article.

11. H. Cantril, H. Gaudet, and H. Herzog, *Invasion from Mars* (Princeton: Princeton University Press, 1940).

12. For a discussion of the feeling of social impotence that marks privatization see E. Kris and N. Leites, "Trends in Twentieth Century Propaganda," in G. Roheim (ed.), *Psychoanalysis and the Social Sciences* (New York: International Universities Press, 1947).

13. For a discussion of the new sense of social responsibility of the press see F. Siebert, T. Peterson, and W. Schramm, *Four Theories of the Press* (Urbana: University of Illinois Press, 1956), Ch. 3.

14. D. Riesman *et. al.*, *The Lonely Crowd* (New York: Doubleday and Company, 1953), Ch. IV.

15. T. W. Adorno, "A Social Critique of Radio Music," *The Kenyon Review*, Vol. VII (1945), pp. 208-217.

CHAPTER TWO

1. F. Siebert, T. Peterson, and W. Schramm, *op. cit.*

2. A. Inkeles, *Public Opinion in Soviet Russia: A Study in Mass Persuasion* (Cambridge: Harvard University Press, 1951).

3. *Basic Facts and Figures* (Paris: Unesco, 1956), addendum to p. 84.

4. *World Communications: Press, Radio, Film, Television* (Paris: Unesco, 1956), p. 120.

5. Inkeles, *op. cit.*, p. 239. Inkeles' estimate refers to 1947 but probably is fairly accurate for later years. Much of our discussion about the Soviet system is derived from information in Inkeles' work, but specific page references are cited only for direct quotations or statistics.

6. *Izvestiya*, November 29, 1933, as quoted in Inkeles, *op. cit.*, p. 227.

7. Inkeles, *op. cit.*, p. 227.

8. *Ibid.*, p. 230.

9. *Ibid.*, pp. 243-244. Data on the cost of receivers is provided by an earlier essay by Inkeles, "Domestic Broadcasting in the U.S.S.R." in Lazarsfeld and Stanton, *op. cit.*, pp. 223-293.

10. Inkeles, "Domestic Broadcasting in the U.S.S.R." p. 256.

11. For a discussion of the impact of Lenin's theories on mass communication see Inkeles, *Public Opinion*, especially Chapters 1 and 2.

12. Information on the Soviet press comes primarily from Inkeles, *op. cit.*, Chapters 9-14.

13. Information on the Soviet film comes from Inkeles, *op. cit.*, Chapter 19, and from *World Communications*, pp. 243-245.

14. C. Siepmann, *Radio, Television and Society* (New York: Oxford University Press, 1950), Chapter VII. Additional statistics are taken from *World Communications*, pp. 220-224.

15. Siepmann, *op. cit.*, pp. 141-154 provides an instructive and detailed discussion of the question of monopoly.

16. J. T. Suchy, "How Does Commercial TV Affect British Viewing?" *Journalism Quarterly*, Winter 1958, pp. 65-71.

17. *Ibid.*

18. Information about the Canadian system comes primarily from Siepmann, *op. cit.*, pp. 154-167.

19. See R. B. Glynn, "The Canadian System," in W. Y. Elliott (ed.), *Television's Impact on American*

Culture (East Lansing: Michigan State University Press, 1956), pp. 109-123.

20. H. Cantril (ed.), *Public Opinion 1935-1946* (Princeton: Princeton University Press, 1951), p. 244.

21. *Ibid.,* pp. 416-418.

22. P. F. Lazarsfeld and P. L. Kendall, *Radio Listening in America* (New York: Prentice-Hall, Inc., 1948), Chapter V.

23. Two works provide the major sources of information on which this section is based: Sydney Head, *Broadcasting in America* (Boston: Houghton Mifflin Company, 1956); and Llewellyn White, *The American Radio* (Chicago: The University of Chicago Press, 1947).

24. White, *op. cit.,* Chapter 7.

25. *Ibid.,* p. 127.

26. Cf. Head, *op. cit.,* Chapter 25.

27. Cf. White, *op. cit.,* Chapter 4.

28. Cf. Head, *op. cit.,* pp. 112-114 and 142-148; also White, *op. cit.,* Chapters 2 and 3.

29. See, e.g., the discussions in Head and in White.

30. Siebert, Peterson, and Schramm, *op. cit.,* p. 7.

31. *Communications Behavior and Political Attitudes in Four Arabic Countries: A Quantitative Comparison* (mimeographed; New York: Bureau of Applied Social Research, 1952). For a summary of parts of this study see E. deS. Brunner, "Rural Communications Behavior and Attitudes in the Middle East," *Rural Sociology,* Vol. 18, No. 2, pp. 149-155. Or see D. Lerner, *The Passing of Traditional Society* (Glencoe, Ill.: Free Press, 1958).

32. Data are from *World Communications*.

33. *Communications Behavior, op. cit.,* pp. 15-16. By permission of the BASR.

34. *Ibid.,* p. 42. By permission of the BASR.

35. For a discussion of the way in which some face-to-face communicators have been given a formal social role in the Soviet communications system see the analysis of oral agitators by Inkeles, *op. cit.*

CHAPTER THREE

1. Herbert Blumer, "Collective Behavior," in A. Lee (ed.), *Principles of Sociology* (New York: Barnes and Noble, Inc., 1946), pp. 185-186. By permission of the publisher. Emphasis supplied.

2. For a fuller discussion of these earlier models of communication, see E. Katz and P. Lazarsfeld, *Personal Influence: The Part Played by People in the Flow of Mass Communications* (Glencoe, Ill.: The Free Press, 1955), Chapters I and II.

3. M. Riley and J. Riley, "A Sociological Approach to Communications Research," *Public Opinion Quarterly*, Vol. 15, No. 3 (Fall 1951), pp. 445-460.

4. L. Handel, *Hollywood Looks At Its Audience* (Urbana: The University of Illinois Press, 1950), pp. 113-115.

5. The analyses of opinion leaders and the two-step flow of communications presented here are based primarily on studies on American audiences. There has been some research on these topics in other societies, but the most extensive work has been done in the United States. The extent to which the American pattern can be generalized to other groups is as yet unknown. For example, it may be that opinion leaders in non-industrial societies are not distributed among all the major social strata, as much as they appear to be within the United States. And even within our own society there is much still to be learned about the *conditions* under which the two-step flow operates—how prevalent it is among various minority groups, at different age levels, and in times of historical' crisis.

6. P. Lazarsfeld, B. Berelson and H. Gaudet, *The People's Choice* (New York: Columbia University Press, 1948). Since all of the findings summarized in this section are derived from this work, specific page references will be cited only for direct quotations.

7. *Ibid.,* p 150. By permission of the publisher.

8. *Ibid.*, p. 50.

9. *Ibid.*, p. xxiii. By permission of the publisher.

10. R. K. Merton, "Patterns of Influence," in Lazarsfeld and Stanton, *op. cit.*, pp. 180-219. The findings summarized in the current section are selected from several parts of the original work.

11. Katz and Lazarsfeld, *op. cit.* Specific page references will be cited only for direct quotations from the study.

12. Lazarsfeld, Berelson, and Gaudet, *op. cit.*

13. Katz and Lazarsfeld, *op. cit.*, p. 185. By permission of the publisher.

14. *Ibid.*, p. 316. By permission of the publisher.

15. Evidence that messages often reach many individuals directly without the mediating efforts of opinion leaders is presented, for example, in a recent voting study by Berelson, Lazarsfeld and McPhee, *Voting* (Chicago: University of Chicago Press, 1954).

16. As an example, see H. Menzel and E. Katz, "Social Relations and Innovation in the Medical Profession: The Epidemiology of a New Drug," *Public Opinion Quarterly*, Vol. 19, No. 4 (Winter 1955-56), pp. 337-352.

17. O. Larsen and R. Hill, "Mass Media and Interpersonal Communication in the Diffusion of a News Event," *American Sociological Review*, 19 (August 1954), pp. 426-443.

18. M. De Fleur and O. Larsen, *The Flow of Information* (New York: Harper and Brothers, 1958). Specific page references will be given only for direct quotations from this work.

19. *Ibid.*, p. 164. By permission of the publisher.

20. *Ibid.*, p. 31. By permission of the publisher.

21. Cf. Lazarsfeld and Kendall, *op. cit.*, Chapter I.

22. Cf. P. Lazarsfeld, "Communications Research and the Social Psychologist," in W. Dennis (ed.), *Current Trends in Social Psychology* (Pittsburgh: The University of Pittsburgh Press, 1948), pp. 249-260.

23. *Ibid.*, pp. 242-244. By permission of the publisher.

CHAPTER FOUR

1. B. Berelson, *Content Analysis in Communication Research* (Glencoe, Ill.: The Free Press, 1952), p. 18.

2. *Ibid.*, Chapter II.

3. L. Lowenthal, "Biographies in Popular Magazines," in Lazarsfeld and Stanton (eds.), *Radio Research, 1942-43* (New York: Duell, Sloan and Pearce, 1943), pp. 507-548.

4. *Ibid.*, pp. 547-548. By permission of the publisher. Copyright 1944.

5. Unpublished paper by K. Poole, graduate student in the Department of Anthropology and Sociology, University of California, Los Angeles.

6. D. Smythe, *Three Years of New York Television* (Monitoring Study Number 6, Urbana, Ill.: National Association of Educational Broadcasters).

7. For further details on semantic differentiation, see C. Osgood, G. Suci, and P. Tannenbaum, *The Measurement of Meaning* (Urbana: University of Illinois Press, 1957).

8. For details on the television audience, see L. Bogart, *The Age of Television* (New York: Frederick Ungar Publishing Company, 1956).

9. These monitoring studies have been published in six volumes by the National Association of Educational Broadcasters, Urbana, Illinois, as follows: D. Smythe and A. Campbell, *Los Angeles Television* (1951); D. Horton, H. Mauksch and K. Lang, *Chicago Summer Television* (1951); D. Smythe, *New York Television, 1951-1952* (1952); D. Smythe, *New Haven Television* (1952); D. Smythe, *Three Years of New York Television* (1953); and The Purdue Opinion Panel (H. Remmers and R. Mainer), *Four Years of New York Television* (1954).

10. The Purdue Opinion Poll, *op. cit.*

11. J. Suchy, *op. cit.*

12. The Purdue Opinion Poll, *op. cit.*, Chapter 6.

13. For an interesting and informative account of ways in which television affects the nature of public events as perceived by the audience, see K. Lang and G. Lang, "The Unique Perspective of Television," *American Sociological Review,* Vol. 18, No. 1, February 1953, pp. 3-12. Also see the Langs' analysis of the manner in which three television networks covered a political convention, "The Inferential Structure of Political Communications: A Study in Unwitting Bias," *Public Opinion Quarterly,* Vol. 19, No. 2 (Summer 1955), pp. 168-183.

14. The Purdue Opinion Poll, *op. cit.*, Chapters 4 and 5.

CHAPTER FIVE

1. P. Lazarsfeld, "Why Is So Little Known About the Effects of TV and What Can Be Done About It," *Public Opinion Quarterly,* Vol. 19, No. 3 (Fall 1955), pp. 243-251.

2. Lazarsfeld and Merton, *op. cit.*

3. Cited in U.S. Congress, Senate Committee on the Judiciary, *Television and Juvenile Delinquency,* Interim Report of the Subcommittee to Investigate Juvenile Delinquency, 84th Congress, 2nd Session (Washington: Government Printing Office, 1956).

4. *Ibid.*

5. F. Wertham, *Seduction of the Innocent* (New York: Rinehart and Company, Inc.), p. 31. By permission of the publisher.

6. E. Maccoby, "Why Do Children Watch Television?" *Public Opinion Quarterly,* Vol. 18, No. 3 (Fall 1954), pp. 239-244.

7. Senate Subcommittee, *op. cit.*

8. Wertham, *op. cit.*, pp. 114-115.

9. For a fuller discussion of socialization as viewed by sociologists, see L. Broom and P. Selznick, *Sociology* (Evanston, Ill.: Row, Peterson and Company, 1958),

Chapter IV; and K. Davis, *Human Society* (New York: Macmillan, 1949), Chapter 8.

10. H. Herzog, "What Do We Really Know About Daytime Serial Listeners?" in Lazarsfeld and Stanton, *op. cit.*, pp. 3-33; Lazarsfeld, "Communications Research and the Social Psychologist," in Dennis, *op. cit.*, pp. 238-239.

11. R. Zajonc, "Some Effects of Space Serials," *Public Opinion Quarterly*, Vol. 18, No. 4 (Winter 1954-1955), pp. 367-374. Raymond Forer, "The Impact of a Radio Program on Adolescents," *Public Opinion Quarterly*, Vol. 19, No. 2 (Summer 1955), pp. 184-194.

12. G. Wiebe, "Merchandising Commodities and Citizenship on Television," *Public Opinion Quarterly*, Vol. 15, No. 4 (Winter 1951-52), p. 684.

13. Kate Smith's marathons have been analyzed scientifically and reported in R. Merton, *Mass Persuasion*, parts of which are summarized later in the chapter.

14. For a fuller account of the campaign and its evaluation, see S. Star and H. Hughes, "Report on an Educational Campaign: The Cincinnati Plan for the United Nations," *American Journal of Sociology*, Vol. LV (January 1950), pp. 389-400.

15. For a fuller discussion see C. Wright, "Evaluating Mass Media Campaigns," *International Social Science Bulletin*, Vol. VII, No. 3 (1955), pp. 417-430.

16. Star and Hughes, *op. cit.*, and National Opinion Research Center Reports No. 37 and 37A, *Cincinnati Looks at the United Nations* and *Cincinnati Looks Again* (mimeographed).

17. H. Hyman and P. Sheatsley, "Some Reasons Why Information Campaigns Fail," *Public Opinion Quarterly*, Vol. II (Fall 1947), pp. 412-423.

18. P. Kendall and K. Wolf, "The Analysis of Deviant Cases in Communications Research," in Lazarsfeld and Stanton, *Communications Research 1948-1949*, pp. 152-179. Cf. E. Cooper and M. Jahoda, "The Evasion of Propaganda: How Prejudiced People Respond to Anti-prejudice Propaganda," *Journal of Psychology*, Vol. 23 (1947), pp. 15-25.

19. As an example, see C. Hovland, A. Lumsdaine, and F. Sheffield, *Experiments on Mass Communication* (Princeton: Princeton University Press, 1949). Other examples can be found in Katz *et al., Public Opinion and Propaganda,* listed under Selected Readings.

20. C. Hovland, I. Janis, and H. Kelley, *Communication and Persuasion* (New Haven: Yale University Press, 1953).

21. C. Hovland and W. Weiss, "Source Credibility and Communication Effectiveness," *Public Opinion Quarterly,* Vol. 15, No. 4 (Winter 1951-1952), pp. 635-650.

22. R. Merton, M. Fiske, and A. Curtis, *Mass Persuasion: The Social Psychology of a War Bond Drive* (New York: Harper and Brothers, 1946).

23. Cf. H. Speier, "Psychological Warfare Reconsidered," in D. Lerner and H. Lasswell (eds.), *The Policy Sciences* (Stanford, Cal.: Stanford University Press, 1951).

24. E. Shils and M. Janowitz, "Cohesion and Disintegration in the Wehrmacht in World War II," *Public Opinion Quarterly,* Vol. 12, No. 2 (Summer 1948), pp. 280-315.

SELECTED READINGS

I. FOUR BOOKS OF READINGS ON MASS COMMUNICATION

Bernard Berelson and Morris Janowitz (eds.), *Reader in Public Opinion and Communication*. Glencoe, Ill.: The Free Press, 1953.

Daniel Katz, Dorwin Cartwright, Samuel Eldersveld and Alfred McClung Lee, *Public Opinion and Propaganda*. New York: Dryden Press, 1954.

Wilbur Schramm, *Mass Communications*. Urbana: University of Illinois Press, 1949.

Wilbur Schramm, *The Process and Effects of Mass Communication*. Urbana: University of Illinois Press, 1954.

II. SPECIAL TOPICS

Functional analysis

Robert K. Merton, *Social Theory and Social Structure*. Glencoe, Ill.: The Free Press, 1957.

Communication systems

Fred Siebert, Theodore Peterson and Wilbur Schramm, *Four Theories of the Press*. Urbana: University of Illinois Press, 1956.

Audiences

Leo Bogart, *The Age of Television*. New York: Frederick Ungar Press, 1956.

Leo Handel, *Hollywood Looks At Its Audience*. Urbana: University of Illinois Press, 1950.

Paul Lazarsfeld and Patricia Kendall, *Radio Listening in America*. New York: Prentice-Hall, 1948.

Opinion Leaders and Personal Influence

Elihu Katz and Paul Lazarsfeld, *Personal Influence*. Glencoe, Ill.: The Free Press, 1955.

Communication Content

Bernard Berelson, *Content Analysis in Communication Research*. Glencoe, Ill.: The Free Press, 1950.

Communication Effects

Carl Hovland, "Effects of the Mass Media of Communication," in Gardner Lindzey (ed.), *Handbook of Social Psychology*. Cambridge, Mass.: Addison Wesley, 1954.

Joseph Klapper, *The Effects of Mass Media*. New York: Bureau of Applied Social Research, Columbia University, 1950.

Selected Research

Paul Lazarsfeld and Frank Stanton (eds.), *Communications Research 1948-1949*. New York: Harper and Brothers, 1949.

Robert K. Merton, Marjorie Fiske and Alberta Curtis, *Mass Persuasion*. New York: Harper and Brothers, 1946.